Stop it. Your Ego is Showing

*How to wrangle in your ego mind and find
the peace you deserve to live as your best self*

EMILY SYRING

ISBN: 978-1-913479-35-0 (paperback)
ISBN: 978-1-913479-36-7 (ebook)

That Guy's House
20-22 Wenlock Road
London
England
N1 7GU

www.ThatGuysHouse.com

That Guy's House

DEDICATION

This is for you. The dreamer. The one with stars in their eyes and big dreams in their heart. You are capable of so much more than you think you are. I believe in you.

CONTENTS

ACKNOWLEDGMENTS

When I was first hit with the idea to write this book and bring it to life, I had every intention of publishing it myself privately and had no idea that in a mere four short weeks I would be part of something so much bigger than I could have ever imagined. The Universe truly had bigger plans for me.

There are no words to express my immense gratitude for the people who helped me make this book possible. Emma Mumford for being my rock and my mentor; pushing me, encouraging me and being by my side through the entire writing process. Sean Patrick, my publisher, and the entire That Guy's House team for the logistics, the editing, and the cover and interior design as well as the immense support and love shown throughout this whole journey.

And my family for sticking with me through all of my ideas. Picking me up when I was down and showing me love, compassion and support throughout this journey.

INTRODUCTION

Sometimes something so big and hairy hops into your lap and smacks you in the face so hard you're pretty sure it left a giant purple bruise. This is the kind of wakeup call I received while sitting in my backyard minding my own business on a perfectly sunny day, picking out the best jelly beans (the pink ones of course) when my "higher self" had the audacity to jump into my lap and call me out on my own bullshit.

I mean come on! All I said was I wasn't cut out for podcasting and no one would like me and my voice is annoying and I'm basically a failure and I should just stick to blogging and no one likes those anyway and I'll never be a writer because I just can't and and and...

"STOP IT YOUR EGO IS SHOWING."

Those six little words sent me hurtling back in my chair so fast you would've thought someone had said something about a video of a pack of puppies playing the piano on the internet and I had fallen out of my chair trying to see them in all their puppy glory. But lucky for me, it was something so much bigger than I could ever have imagined. That was the day I decided to stop living small, wipe away my excuses, and choose to live a bigger life. As cheesy as it sounds, that's the day that changed the course of my life forever. It's also the day I decided to write this book but my story begins much further back than that. So, who even am I?

The girl behind the book. The girl with the chatty ego. I am Emily Syring and I am a woman with a really big dream and the tenacity to go after it regardless of what that little voice inside my head has to say about it. But let's just be honest here, I wasn't always like that. I know what it's like to live inside your own head. Hiding from the world, putting yourself down, believing everything is rigged against you - but at the same time, being afraid of living a mediocre life. I'm here to empower you to get out of your own head and step into your power. Whether you know it's there yet or not.

I am an author, a blogger, an NLP practitioner and life coach specializing in mindset, The Law of Attraction and manifestation. I am also 100%, deeply and completely, in love with learning. As cliché as that might sound. My story begins as a little girl, sitting in my bedroom perched on my window seat scribbling furiously in my little fuzzy purple journal. I can still feel that plush pink and white polka dotted cushion underneath my butt as I now sit in my own backyard, gazing out at my dog hopping about trying to catch a bumble bee while I try to concentrate long enough to write this book.

Even as a young child I knew I would be a writer. I spent my days in my bedroom creating and writing whatever my little mind could come up with. Love stories, action and adventure, Sci-Fi. I loved it all. Little did I know a tiny fearful voice inside my head had other plans for me. But I was too busy romping around the playground, sipping my blueberry blast juice box, asking dad for a soda on a Monday even though I was only allowed soda on Fridays and mom had already said no, all while rocking out to the Backstreet Boys from the CD in my boombox, to even notice.

My real ego story begins like any other teenager going through puberty in the 21st century. Comparing my body to overly photoshopped models, taking what the most popular girl in high school said about me as the truth, the whole truth, and nothing but the truth. And sabotaging any and every chance of putting myself out there because, "What if they don't like me?", "What if they judge me?", "What if they make fun of me?"

Who the heck is "they" anyway?

You would think as you get older these thoughts, fears and self-deprecating words would just fall away and you'd grow up. At least that's what we were taught in health class anyway. But here's the thing about the mind, it only changes when you choose to change it. And you only choose to change it when you realize there's something there to change. Catch 22 anyone?

This is why when I spent years trying to change everything on the outside, blaming everyone and everything that got in my way, and drowning my sorrows in a bottle of wine every night, nothing changed. Much to my own dismay. It wasn't until I took a long hard look at what I was saying and how I was saying it to myself that the wheels started to turn in my favor. I'm pretty sure there's even a 90's song named after this phenomenon but I'll just say this, we are truly our own worst enemies.

Here's what really happened when I got older and grew up. That internal "mean girl" inside my head got louder, and bossier, but she never really seemed to grow up. It was like she was running the show as my child self. She got so loud in fact I spent most of my twenties living a double life. The life outside my head, and the one inside of it. And when I wasn't living inside my head, I was looking for something or someone to fill the dark and vast void curling up in my life like a burly black bear hunkering down for the polar vortex. Yeah, she's sticking around for a while.

I sabotaged relationships that got "too complicated"; "oh you like me too much? Oh, we're getting too comfortable with each other? Not gonna work. See ya." I used food as a physical cork to fill the ever-growing void and when the food alone didn't work, I grabbed a bottle (or two or three) of wine to try and drown out the sound of the voice inside my head. Which never worked for long enough and just left me with a pounding headache, a bloated belly, and a slew of text messages on my phone I never remembered sending.

I even stayed in unfulfilling jobs and relationships long after they had expired. I overlooked red flags, nay, comically large flashing red light bulbs with the word RUN plastered across them. I lived a life of fake smiles and pretending I had my shit together on the outside while the inside of my head ran around yelling and screaming with two brightly colored throw pillows in each hand, about anything and everything that was bound to keep me stuck like quick sand right where I was.

I desperately wanted more, but every time I even thought about sliding a toe outside of the penalty line, that voice inside my head would pipe up and make sure I would slink back into my old ways. It was like having that "one parent" at every sporting event that thought the ref was an idiot and called the shots like they owned the place, running my life from inside my brain.

"THAT WAS OBVIOUSLY A FOUL!" "DON'T YOU KNOW YOU CAN'T RUN AWAY FROM YOUR COMFORT ZONE?" "GET BACK IN HERE NOW!"

These words were all masked by the sound of, "I'm doing this because I want to keep you safe. And I care about you."

So, I believed it.

And believe me when I say choosing a life outside of that cushy place we like to call the "comfort zone" is one of the toughest decisions you will ever have to make. It's about as difficult as choosing a restaurant to eat at when you're really hungry but just don't know what you're hungry for. And the thing is, your ego will do everything in its power to keep you living small the minute you decide you want something more out of life.

Whether that be sending in the negative Nancies and every naysayer on your block, turning off your internet right before finalizing that big presentation, or yelling so loudly in your ear you actually begin to believe what she's saying and begin questioning every move you make.

Even family, friends and strangers you don't even know will come out of the woodwork and try to push their limiting beliefs and stories onto you.

"Are you sure you want to break up with your boyfriend because there are no nice guys around here for miles and you don't want to end up like your great aunt Suzie." Or, "Don't you think it's an awful idea to take out a loan to build that business even if it is your dream? It'll probably fail in the first year anyway. I mean that's what all the magazines say." Or, "Don't write that book. Someone else has already written something similar and they actually have a degree. I mean you didn't even go to college."

If your ego thinks it will stop you, it will do it. This is why most people live a life less than fulfilling and why I chose to drown my sorrows in a bottle of wine every single night instead of ya know, chasing after my dreams and building a business I'd be proud to slap my name on. Among other things. I listened to my ego and what she had to say over what I really wanted and knew I was capable of. And I did this for years.

Because going against yourself is like staring a snarling, spitting pack of wolves in the face and jumping right into the middle of them with your eyes shut tight, screaming the entire way through and just hoping that you make it out the other side. Which you will, by the way.

It's scary as all hell, there are going to be people who will think you're nuts, you're going to second guess yourself and you might even end up with a salty, mascara-stained pillowcase at the end of the night. But on the other side of all that is a life grander than you could ever image.

There's a reason there's a saying about the life you've always wanted begins on the other side of your comfort zone, or something like that. It's because if you want to continue living the life you're living right now, listen to your ego; if you want to live the life that you know you're supposed to be living, choose to ignore your ego and go after it.

You may have picked up this book simply because of the title and expected it to be about big burly men talking about their muscles and you wanted a good laugh, or maybe you simply wanted to learn more about this so-called ego that's holding you back from living your best life.

Whatever the reason, you know you want to live large and in charge and in order to do that you need to get an understanding of the ego mind. Because once you understand it, you can begin to work with it instead of allowing it to run the show. While I am a sucker for science, this book isn't about fancy graphs or brain and psychology experts. It's about your ego mind and your higher self as well as my own personal journey of "who will prevail in the game of 'the king in the mountain' inside my head." And you're reading a book about it so you can probably guess who came out on top and who was left bruised and bloodied down below.

This book isn't about waking up one day, looking in the mirror and seeing that 45 pounds of pure fat had melted off of me like an ice cube in the Mojave Desert. Or all of a sudden having 10 million dollars in the bank appear from an unknown source and being an overnight success, well, overnight. Simply put, this is not a "get rid of your ego quick scheme". It's about getting clear on what's holding you back from living the big incredible life you can only daydream about while sifting through paper work at your soul crushing day job and then jumping in the middle of this big incredible life you have planned for yourself, parachute or no parachute.

If you want to live a bigger life, learn to run the show and are willing to take a deep look inside yourself, this book, and you, have all the tools you need to do so. Your best life begins from the inside out and that's where your success story starts. Right here and right now, make the conscious decision to be open minded (pun intended), willing to air out your dirty laundry, and choose to tackle the ego mind head on, shoulder pads and all.

CHAPTER 1

You'll get there a whole lot faster if you ask for directions

You don't have to know everything to start something, but you do need to know where you are and where you're going. If you're reading this book then you know your ego is basically in control of your life, or you think she is, and you're ready to take life by the horns and make some really big changes around here. You also know that you'll get to your destination a whole heck of a lot faster if you stop and ask for directions, or at least use a GPS or something. And yes, I am referring to this book as your GPS.

At this point, you're probably thinking you want to rid yourself of your ego like an old pair of dirty, ripped up jeans and just forget about it, because you may be thinking that where you want to go is some place where your ego isn't hiding, waiting to pounce. . And I know, the ego gets such a bad rap, but I mean, all she's really trying to do is keep you alive.

I wish I could sit here and tell you that after everything, my ego has pulled an "Elvis" and left the building but it hasn't. I have just learned how to hear what she has to say, dismantle her fears and outcries by poking very large holes in her fears and outcries and move on with my life by showing up even bigger and bolder than I did before. I still feel the fear but I choose to keep moving forward anyway. If you've ever heard the saying, "new level, new devil" then you know what I'm talking about. Feeling fear is part of the human experience, but you can learn how to use it to your advantage instead of allowing it to control every move you make.

Here's the kicker; your ego is slippery, slick and goes wherever your attention goes. She just happens to be the most pessimistic person in the room. As I said previously, she's sticking around no matter what because we biologically need her to survive. It's your job to learn to live with her instead of allowing her to live your life for you. So no, the goal of this book is not to get rid of the ego all together, slam the door shut and go frolicking in a field of dandelions on a hot July day.

This book serves as your guide to recognize the ego when she comes up, to teach you how to dismantle her when what she's saying isn't helping you, and to learn how to ask yourself the right questions to simply quiet your ego mind so that you can go after what you want while showing up as the best possible version of yourself. No matter what you are doing now or how successful you are right now or how successful you will become, your ego will always pop up. It's my job to equip you with the best tools to overcome your ego and it's your job to show up for yourself and do the work.

When you're driving to a destination you've never been, it's a whole hell of a lot easier to get there if you stop and ask for directions. Even if just while you're reading this book you allow that analogy to soak in it will make a world of difference. Stay in the question, be open minded, and keep your seat belt on -this is going to be a bumpy ride.

Be Open to Receiving

Whether you've always been someone who does it on their own or you simply don't like asking for help (at least for the time being), let that story go and be open to receiving. This book is going to force you to crack open your stories and put them on full display. You may notice you come across a few things you've heard before and your ego might tell you to just skip that part because you "know" it already. Once again, I encourage you to suspend your stories, suspend everything you already know, and be as open as possible to receiving the information provided in this book.

How to get the most out of this book:

1. I'm going to guess that this isn't the first personal development or mindset book that you've ever picked up in your life. Maybe you've read a few here and there, maybe thousands, or maybe you've bought hundreds but have never even cracked the cover open. If you got this far, I applaud you.

    But this book and your best life are going to need something from you. They are going to need you to be committed to not only finishing this book but also doing the work.

- Before you go any further, ask yourself these three questions:

- Who do I need to be to finish this book? (what characteristics do you need?)
- Where do I want to be after reading this book?
- What do I want to get out of this book?
- How do I want to feel after reading this book?

    Set an intention to be open minded to the concepts presented to you in this book. Yes, this *is* really important because this is basically giving your mind a direction to listen up, pay attention, and be open to what is being said.

    To set an intention, simply say out loud or in your head, "I choose to be open minded and willing to learn while reading this book." That's it.

2. Read this book multiple times. Every single time you read something, you end up picking up a new piece of information that you didn't see before which is why it's so crucial for you to read this book over and over and over again.

I encourage you to also come back to this book and go through the action steps and the journal prompts any time you notice your ego coming up. This will help you get in the habit of working through your ego's thoughts and fears instead of letting them control your every move. Making new habits requires repetition.

3. Ask yourself questions and do the work. I can't do the work for you, that is up to you. If you notice yourself reading a chapter and you notice you are dismissing it, get present to the story you have around what is being said.. Make sure you actually take the time to go through the journal prompts at the end of each chapter.

These are very important questions and will help you get a better understanding of your ego mind on a personal level. The point is to stay in the question, and become aware of the stories popping up as you read through this book because that, my friend, is the work.

"My ego likes to whisper stories in my ear of the "what if's" and what will happen if I choose poorly. And when she's finished, I say, "Not today. I choose to see it differently."

CHAPTER 2

WHAT IS YOUR EGO AND WHO THE HECK INVITED HER?

I personally love to personify the ego mind and will continue to do so throughout this book. I give her a personality, a cute little outfit, the whole nine. Simply because this makes it easier for me to understand her and frankly, ignore her to do my own thing with this one life we're all so graciously given.

It also makes it easier for me to see her as less of an outside entity but more as a voice that's just living small and afraid that is simply part of me and everyone else. I also choose to see her as neither good nor bad. She just *is*. So, what even really is your ego mind and why in the world do we even have one if she's so mean spirited and basically out here to just ruin our good time?

We love to pretend the ego mind is this big evil thing that's completely separate from us, but in reality, its sole purpose is to simply keep us safe. Your ego mind is that part of your brain that acts on your flight or fight response to uh, ya know, keep you alive and such.

We all have one and we all come fully intact with them as soon as we're born. The ego mind is neither good nor bad but just takes its job very seriously and will do whatever it needs to do to keep our hearts pumping and blood flowing, even if that means making us live a life that makes us stand around the water cooler praying for 5 o' clock to come. I mean come on, it was 3 o' clock like four hours ago.

The ego comes in quite handy when you're alone walking down a dimly lit alley at 2am, while dark shadow creatures with glowing orbs for eyes peer at you from their nightly feed in the trash. The ego is not so helpful however, when you look at a dollar bill and feel an impending urge to scream, cry, throw something or curl into a ball of regret. Or when you get cut off in traffic by a man three times your size sporting a beautifully tattooed snake around his neck, and decide his heinous act of cutting you off is worth losing a few teeth over.

You see, your ego mind is simply there to protect you. Its only job is to keep you alive, which sounds like a pretty great thing to me. It only becomes a problem when we allow it to control our every move and keep us playing small. The goal is not to completely quiet the ego mind but simply to understand her and question everything she's saying. Then go out and do what we know we need to do to live that big life we want to live.

So, who the heck invited her? Why do we even have an ego mind and will there ever be a generation without one? This question was brought up over lunch by my adoring and beautiful mom and I had to wonder this myself. The fact of the matter is, we would not be here today if it weren't for our egos.

You see, your ego mind was developed all those years ago when the first humans walked the earth. Back then the ego mind worked wonders in keeping our species alive and well. Although, in those days the real dangers were saber tooth tigers piercing off our loincloths and getting stomped on by a woolly mammoth or whatever. If you wanted to live, you had to either fight or run screaming for your life and hope that the snarling pack of saber tooth tigers wasn't trailing behind you.

The same rang true for living in a pack or family or whatever we called them back then. If you were shunned, pushed out of the cave or left behind, this basically meant death. This is why it's so difficult for us to stand out, rebel against loved ones and take the road less traveled; the fear is still there even if the real danger isn't.

Fast forward a couple thousand years to the great depression era. Our subconscious mind is evolving and absorbing brand new beliefs. The beliefs that money is scarce, there's not enough for everyone, fend for yourself. These beliefs are simply stories created by thoughts that create feelings inside of us. When we feel scared our brain looks for a reason why we're afraid: there's no food, there's no money to buy food, people are taking the money away - people are evil, money is evil, so people with money are evil.

These beliefs are then put into our heads by our parents and the people around us by the words they use, their body language, their emotions and so on. Our subconscious mind then stores these beliefs and creates actions to make them true. Our ego then takes these beliefs and turns them into who we are. If we believe money is the root of all evil, our ego says that's just who we are and pushes us to take the necessary actions to keep us away from money.

So, we turn into someone who is always broke and afraid of money even if our only desire is to run a multi-million-dollar empire. The ego also doesn't understand real world problems or problems of the 21st century, and it doesn't really care; what it does care about is our life. So, the ego does everything in its power to keep us away from the things we fear and the things we created as our identities.

If you look at a puppy and feel fear, your ego is going to create thoughts based on that feeling of fear to keep you away from puppies. And it does this with anything we feel we need to fight or be afraid of. Your ego is simply reacting to your own emotional reactions and because you cannot have a thought without an emotion, whether it be neutral, pure terror, joy, sadness etc., our ego is always working and always speaking up.

The ego also loves to tell us who we are, and who we are *not* based on past experiences.

"I am someone who only attracts men that cheat because that's what happened five years ago", "I am someone who cannot run their own business because six months ago I couldn't even talk to potential clients".

You see, the ego loves the past and pretends to be the world's greatest fortune teller. If you can always predict what will happen based on past events, then you will always be prepared for whatever is to come. Makes sense, right? We just don't need that type of thinking for everything. Your ego also doesn't care what you look like, how much money you make, or if you help little old ladies cross the street. It just wants to keep your blood pumping through your veins which means keeping you safely tucked away in your comfort zone of inaction.

If it happened before, it'll happen again because that's just who you are. You probably notice that you repeat the same patterns over and over again. This is simply the ego identifying you as someone who does that based on the past. And if you choose to listen to the ego you will get the same result over and over and over again. Why? Because knowing what's going to happen is safe.

"If I just sit on my couch all day I don't have to deal with strangers. I don't have to be afraid. It's safe here."

There's safety in knowing. It's the unknown outcomes that scare the living shit out of the ego, which is why it's crucial to use the unknown to your full advantage.

Here's another thing about the ego mind; it's sneaky and is a master of disguise. Your ego can sneak up in the form of conceit, being the loudest person in the room, making everyone else happy before yourself, jealousy, pushing others around, being a "yes person", and the most obvious - pure, unadulterated fear. The reality is, whether we're aware of it or not, all of these emotions stem from fear.

The fear of not being heard, the fear of being forgotten, the fear of not having what everyone else has, the fear of losing someone we love, the fear of success or failure. And the ego mind thrives on fear. That's where it gets all of its juice and power. Because fear keeps us from taking action. Plain and simple. When we don't take action, we're "safe". At least according to the ego mind. But the ego mind doesn't just tell you what not to do, it also justifies why you're staying stuck in a situation that would make other people scream.

"Why are you with him when he treats you so poorly?" "Because his behaviour is familiar to me."

What you're really saying is, it's more comfortable to stay with him than it is to put myself out there into the world of dating and possibly get rejected. Or, it's scarier to be alone than to be with someone who cheats on me. The fear is bigger than the reward and that is what the ego is counting on.

Overcoming your ego mind doesn't always require giant leaps of faith into the unknown (although that is the case sometimes), it simply takes the decision to recognize it when it's coming up for you and to choose not to listen to it. But if you really want to send your ego back to her corner with her tail tucked between her legs then it requires doing something that scares you.

For you this may mean starting that blog you've always wanted to start, doing your first video on social media or even leaving the house for the first time today. Everyone's comfort zone looks different. This isn't about comparing yourself to someone else. Or thinking you haven't done enough. It's about recognizing what patterns and behaviors have gotten you to where you are today, recognizing the voice of your ego, and making the conscious decision to take a different path.

The path of, well, resistance. At least at first. Then with more practice, you'll begin to notice the areas of your life that your ego is controlling. You will be able to listen to her objectively and then move on. Remember, your ego is not something to fear, she is a part of you and you get to choose how you react or not react to her.

"Instead of running away from your problems, run towards their solution."

CHAPTER 3

YOUR SUBCONSCIOUS MIND, THE KEEPER OF YOUR SECRETS

In the previous chapter you learned that there is an ego part of your mind, also known as your reptilian brain, which is basically the oldest part of your brain, and the sole purpose of your ego is to keep you safe in your comfort zone. Here's the thing though; most of what the ego does is on a subconscious level, meaning you don't always consciously think about what you're doing. You may hear your ego speak up but the actions and behaviors that you take based on your ego are on a subconscious level.

If you want to understand how to overcome your ego and the role it plays in your life, you also have to understand what your subconscious mind is and what it does because yes, it is all subconscious. And 90-95% of people are running their lives on autopilot, meaning they are living subconsciously and their actions, behaviors, thoughts and beliefs are all running on autopilot as well.

Alarm goes off, get up, shower, eat breakfast, run out the door, work, work, work, work, drive home, watch tv, go to bed.

Wake up and do it all over again. And throughout the day we have subconscious thoughts that pop up based on what is going on around us. And the way we react to these things is based on our subconscious programming which is created as children. So, if you're running life on autopilot, this means you will get the same results over and over and over again, no matter what you try to change externally. Even if you consciously want to change.

But why though? Why does this happen? I mean come on, on a conscious level you may think and truly believe that you want to change. That you want to make the kind of changes that make your eyes water and overflow with happiness. And yet you find yourself sabotaging the whole thing, by eating a dozen donuts every single day, cheating on your boyfriend or skipping the mindset work. All this just leaves you with more questions, taking the same actions you've always taken, thinking the same thoughts you've always thought, and living the same life you've always lived.

Frustrating right? So why then does this happen? Well, it all comes down to our subconscious mind which is, in essence, the filter in which you see the world determining the results you will see in your physical reality. And whatever beliefs, thoughts, and emotions have been programmed into your subconscious mind will be the filter in which you take the actions that create the results you see in your external reality.

External Situation ——> Thoughts/emotions and feelings ——-> A story is formed which is also a Belief ——> Creates the Actions you take that Align with that Belief = Your Physical Reality.

To break this down even further, an external situation happens which we absorb as information, the subconscious mind then deletes, distorts, or generalizes the information or situation based on internal filters such as time and location, your mood, your beliefs, values, and identity. This then creates a thought in your conscious mind, which *then* creates an emotion/feeling and a meaning about what that external situation means about who you are. This creates a belief which creates the actions that align with those beliefs. Your actions then create your external reality and the results you see physically. Remember, this is all happening on a subconscious level meaning we are not even aware that this all happening at any given time throughout the day. Which is great because this is a lot.

Your subconscious mind takes in 2.3 billion bits per second of information throughout the day but luckily our brain has a way of sorting and sifting through this information subconsciously for us. The Reticular Activating System, or RAS, takes on the billions of bits of information we collect throughout any given day and creates a filter for us based on the information that we decided was of value to us based on our attention.

Think of your subconscious mind kind of like a social media algorithm. When you interact with someone's post, in a positive or negative way (commenting, liking, sharing etc.), the platform will begin to show you more of those types of posts and will specifically show you more posts from that person simply because the algorithm believes that whatever posts you give attention to, you want to see more of. Regardless of if the attention you were giving was negative or positive. And the algorithm doesn't stop showing you these types of posts until you physically tell it not to.

Your RAS does the same thing. Wherever your attention is placed is what you will see more of. Which is why when you think about ice cream, you see it everywhere. Because your RAS is filtering in anything to do with ice cream and searching for ice cream to show you. And it will do this even with things you may or may not want to see simply because it's based on your attention.

The Reticular Activating System is also responsible for validating your beliefs and will filter out anything that does not align with those beliefs. It is literally programmed to work in your favor and will find any and all information to prove that you are right. Which means, if you consciously want to change something in your physical reality, such as wanting more money, but have contradicting beliefs programmed on a subconscious level, your RAS will filter out anything that doesn't align with those old beliefs. Which can make changing your life on a physical level very difficult.

This is also why self-sabotage is the leading cause of not living your best damn life. Because your ego will have you believe that the only way to live your best life is to do the things that you know how to do, i.e. stay where you're comfortable, work harder, work longer, do all the physical action type things. And your RAS is just following orders on a subconscious level.

This is also why motivation and willpower will only get you so far before your subconscious will take over and push you back into a place that aligns with your identity, values, and beliefs. If you want to make lasting changes, you will have to program your mind on a subconscious level to align with the life that you want.

So how does your ego come into all this? The voice of your ego is also programmed based on your past thoughts, beliefs, and actions and uses the past to predict future outcomes and keep you safe and alive. Your ego is literally your inner dialogue. The voice you hear on a conscious level. But it's really just speaking up based on what's programmed in your subconscious mind.

I realize this all sounds overcomplicated, frustrating, and downright terrifying but it's not. And really, it's just your ego speaking up and trying to pretend like doing something new is more painful than trying to do something that may actually help you live the life you've always dreamed about living.

Your subconscious mind is just doing its job. We will be taking a deep dive into reprogramming, challenging, and changing your subconscious beliefs but for now, I want you to understand just how powerful your subconscious mind actually is.

There are many jobs of the subconscious mind and some of them include: preserving the body and keeping you alive, and storing and organizing all of your memories. Yes, every single one. The subconscious mind holds your emotions, maintains your habits, and loves to do things quickly. Which is why it likes to take the path of least resistance. Because doing something you already know how to do takes less time than learning how to do something new. Your subconscious mind also loves pictures and images to understand the world. Quick! Think of a purple elephant! Even though you've never seen one, you know what purple looks like and you know what an elephant looks like so your subconscious mind puts the two together and creates an image. Pretty cool right?

One thing to remember though is that your subconscious mind doesn't recognize or process negatives. It needs to create an image first to be able to understand. It can't not think of a "not" purple elephant without first thinking of a purple elephant. This is why it's so important to put a heavy focus on what you want, not what you don't want.

Your subconscious mind is extremely powerful and is essentially a GPS system searching for the easiest way to accomplish something. The thing is, what's programmed into your subconscious mind are beliefs, values, and identities that often do not belong to you because they were instilled in you when you were a child. It's your responsibility as an adult to recognize the beliefs that no longer serve you and type in a new destination into your GPS system. The new destination is outside of your comfort zone which is why your ego speaks up so much.

"Some lessons come in small packages but if you're too busy looking for the big ones, you might just miss them."

CHAPTER 4

YOUR EGO VS YOUR HIGHER SELF: WHO WILL WIN IN THE BATTLE OF YOUR LIFE?

It's hard enough realizing there's a voice inside your head trying to keep you living in your comfort zone with the same gusto as someone trying to walk six dogs of varying sizes all at the same time. But there's actually a second voice fighting for space in there and this is what we call our "higher selves", also known as your intuition. What in the world is this "higher self" voice, and is she trying to keep you living small too?

Thankfully no. Your higher self is basically your biggest cheerleader, your biggest fan, and the voice rooting for you to live the biggest possible life you can think of and then some. Your higher self is also the part of you that puts those big dreams into your heart. Seriously, they wouldn't be there if it wasn't possible for you to achieve them. Your higher self comes from a place of love and compassion and always has your best interest at heart. Your higher self/intuition can be described as a feeling you get when you know something is off or when something is perfect for you. It's your gut instinct and it's always right. I also like to think of your higher self as less living in your head and more in your heart.

Sometimes, your higher self comes to you via a voice inside your head and sends you the right messages at the exact right time and other times it's simply a feeling you get. When I get these feelings, they tend to start in my stomach and then if I don't listen to the feeling, I'll hear a voice telling me what I need to do. It just takes practice to understand where you feel your higher self/intuition the most in your body because everyone is so different.

The kicker is that both of these voices sound exactly like you. So how are you supposed to decipher between the two? Let's break down these two voices to get a clear understanding of how they speak and interact in your head.

Ego Mind

- **Child like**
- **Likes instant gratification**
- **Impulsive**
- **Comes from a place of fear**
- **Uses fear to keep you stuck, or at least feeling stuck**
- **Lives in the past and future to decide if something should be feared or not**
- **Does everything in its power to keep you inside your comfort zone and a place it knows the outcome**
- **Creates an identity for you based on past experiences and uses inaction to keep you "safe"**
- **Only sees the problem instead of the solution.**

Higher Self/Intuition

- **Your adult self – minus social norms and past experiences**

- **Lives in the present moment**
- **Sees the big picture**
- **Comes from a place of love and compassion**
- **Always has your best interest at heart**
- **Loves action and lessons to keep you moving forward**
- **Understands you have feelings and emotions but does not identify you by them**
- **Only sees the solution and only focuses on the problem long enough to find a solution.**
- **Initial gut feeling and instinct on what to do and if it feels right.**
- **Is plugged directly into Source**

Essentially, the ego is always working out of fear to keep you where you are and in a familiar place, and your higher self is always working with love and compassion to get you to where you want to be. It's up to you to decide which voice is speaking when you have a big speaking gig coming up and you feel like you might pass out, throw up, or pee yourself. Chances are, if you are feeling uncomfortable and you're about to do something that's unfamiliar to you, it's your ego's voice that will be the loudest in the room.

Another way to decipher between your ego mind and your intuition is to tap into the feelings you're getting from what's coming up. If you are feeling frantic, jittery, or intense fear, this is coming from your ego as the ego's energy is more "aggressive". Whereas when a message from your intuition comes up it can be a small feeling such as something just not feeling right - but it holds a much calmer energy. This will take practice to learn which voice is speaking and which one isn't.

Let's talk about that higher self/intuition voice a bit more to get an even better understanding of her and why she is so important to listen to if we want to show up bigger and bolder in our daily lives. The fact of the matter is this; you were put on this earth to play a bigger game. You were put here for a reason. It wasn't luck, it wasn't a coincidence. As far as what that reason is though, I can't tell you because that's for you to find out.

When you look at your life and think you really want to be an influencer in some capacity, or you want to devote your life to giving the homeless better lives, or raising really amazing, compassionate, creative kids, it's because those thoughts and desires were put into you by your higher self, source, the universe, God. Those ideas simply wouldn't have been put in your head and heart unless they were what you were supposed to do.

I will be diving deeper into these types of concepts later on in this book but the idea that you're here to just sip scalding hot coffee by a water cooler while rolling your eyes at your boss's latest fishing story, avoiding speaking up when you have something to say, or staying in relationships that keep you small and miserable, is simply an act of your ego mind.

You are not single handedly trying to win at the game of life, there is something else on your team and once you recognize this, things in life become a million times easier. While your ego uses past experiences as an identity of who you are today, your higher self uses lessons in the moment to keep you moving in the right direction. Listening to the ego is like sitting in a car and knowing exactly where you want to go but choosing to just sit there in the parking lot.

Sure, it'll keep you safe right where you are, you won't have to do anything scary or uncomfortable, but you really won't get anywhere either. And you'll just keep reliving the same patterns over and over again. Listening to your higher self is like getting in the car, typing your destination into your GPS and driving with complete and utter faith that you'll end up at your desired destination. Yeah, you may hit a few pot holes, run into a few construction sites and have to reroute a few times but you will get there with the lessons you need for right now and the future.

Frankly, you can't get to where you're going if you're not moving. And most of the places you want to get to are unfamiliar territory for you, otherwise you probably wouldn't be where you are. That's the difference- your higher self sees the unknown as something exciting because it means you're doing something you've never done before and going to places you've never been. Your ego sees the unknown as something to be feared because it cannot predict the outcome.

Now sticking with the car analogy, let's put your ego and your higher self in the same car. Think back to when you were a kid. If you have kids now, then you can probably guess how this is going to go. Your ego is throwing Cheetos at your higher self while your higher self is trying to get into the right turn lane and when the Cheeto throwing, yelling and screaming doesn't work your ego takes it upon herself to rip off her seat belt and put her foot on the break. All while your higher self has her foot on the gas pedal.

So what ends up really happening is you move three feet forward then have the brakes slammed on you, then you move another two feet, then the brake pedal is slammed on again, making you come to a screeching halt. If you're lucky, maybe you get another ten feet forward before your ego once again sticks a giant big toe onto the brake pedal of your life.

I'm sure I'm not the first person to tell you that life is a long journey and the roads are winding with some really beautiful scenery. The last thing you need is a Cheeto throwing, screaming at the top of her lungs, brake pedal pushing ego cramping your style the whole trip there. The common thought here to quiet your ego would be to put your headphones on and blast the music. Or in my case, take a nice long scroll down Instagram lane while drinking wine, and fill up my brain with other people's lives instead of dealing with the problem of my ego.

All your ego wants is to be heard. She just wants to know that yeah, you get it. Sometimes not knowing the outcome is scary, life can be tough but it doesn't have to be. It's your job to hear her, let her say her peace, understand what thoughts and feelings are coming up and then create new ones that give you a solution. As soon as you honor her voice, she backs off the brake pedal and you're on your way again.

Let's break this down one more step again, using the car. Your ego is yelling, your higher self is in control of the wheel, but you have one foot on the gas and one foot on the brake. Making you speed up a bit, then slow down, and sometimes even come to a full-blown stop. Instead of ignoring your ego completely begin to ask yourself a few questions to help give voice to your ego:

Has this problem come up in the past?

Yes.

Are you better equipped with new solutions to overcome this problem than you were before?

Yes.

Thank your ego and move forward knowing you have all the answers you need to overcome any problem that may arise.

Let's rework this the other way. If this problem has not come up in the past before and it's something brand new:

Has this problem come up in the past?

No.

Do you have the internal resources (you do, trust me) to ask questions, brainstorm, and aid you in overcoming this problem?

Yes.

Move forward trusting that you already have everything you need to have everything you want. And you have all the internal resources to overcome any problem that comes your way.

Here's the thing, your ego and your higher self see problems in two very different ways. Your ego sees a problem and immediately wants to run from it, cover it up, pretend it's not there, deal with it later, or decide there is no solution. Your higher self sees a problem just long enough to figure out the solution. And by asking yourself the right questions as soon as you notice your ego pushing on the brakes, you are allowing your higher self to regain control and begin to poke holes in the story your ego is trying to tell you.

But asking yourself the right questions isn't always the easiest thing to do because, you guessed it, most people are asking questions from the ego's perspective which means you're getting answers that keep you stuck and only align with the filters (beliefs, thoughts, feelings and actions) that are programmed into your subconscious mind.

On the plus side, analyzing the questions you are asking can be an easy way to figure out which voice is controlling your life. Not only that but the questions you ask can be the biggest determining factor in what you will see as a physical outcome. Meaning, if you ask yourself the right questions, you'll get the right answers which will give you a new outcome.

QUESTIONS FROM YOUR EGO:	QUESTIONS FROM YOUR INTUITION:
• What if I fail?	• What if I succeed?
• Why is this happening to me?	• What is the best that can happen?
• How much will that cost me?	• What can I learn from this situation?
• What if they hate me?	• What is this trying to teach me?
• Why does this work for everyone else except me?	• Why am I feeling this way about x, y, z?
• Why is this so hard and heavy and challenging?	• Is this the truth?
• Can you guarantee I will get those results?	• Can I change the story I am telling myself?
• Why is everything so expensive?	• How can I find a solution?
• Why is everyone better at this than me?	• Is this investment worth my time?
• Why does this ALWAYS happen to me?	• What is the solution to this?
• What am I doing wrong?	• Who do I need to be or become to make this work?
• I'm doing everything right, why isn't this working for me?	• Where do I need to work on this?
• Why is everyone else so much further along than me?	• Okay, that didn't work. What can I do differently next time?
	• What does this goal need from me?

Of course, there are many other types of questions that come more from the ego than from intuition but for the most part, the questions that come from your ego keep you stuck, and the questions that come from your intuition give you the answers that maybe you don't really want to hear but need to hear. They are also the types of answers that will propel you forward.

This also allows your ego to be heard and gives you the insight you need the next time a similar problem occurs again. Because when you can get to the root cause of why your ego is speaking up, then you will begin to notice it as soon as it happens and rewrite the story before your ego mind takes hold.

Journal Prompts

As I said, asking yourself questions is one of the many ways to decipher between your ego and your higher self/intuition, but the thing is, most people are asking the wrong questions. As with anything else, asking the right questions takes practice and the more you do it, the better and easier it will become. Below are a few questions you can ask yourself now to get a clearer picture of how your ego and higher self show up in your life.

1. Have you been making the majority of your decisions in life from your ego or your higher self?
2. Why do you think that is?
3. How do you personally identify your higher self or intuition? Where do you feel it in your body? Or do you hear a voice in your head?
4. How does listening to your ego feel? How does listening to your higher self/intuition feel?
5. Are you ready to make the commitment to listen to your higher self over your ego?

"Your ego leads with fear. Your higher self leads with love and wisdom."

CHAPTER 5

SHOWING UP FOR YOURSELF
IS NON NEGOTIABLE

"I'm not mad, I'm just disappointed".

I can still see my parents' faces hanging low, with furrowed brows and crossed arms when I told them I got a D in math class. To be completely honest, I wasn't even the slightest bit bothered by this D (even though I knew I could do better) but just the look of disappointment was enough for me to feel a small sliver of shame for not trying just a little bit harder. Even if trying harder meant dividing fractions and ya know, paying attention in class instead of drooling over boys and scribbling in my notebook. Not to mention taking the time to rid myself of the story I threw at anyone and everyone who asked that sounded something like;

"I'm not good at math. Math is hard. Therefore, getting anything above an F is good enough for me."

I paint this picture because I think you can easily relate to it. And those six little words, "I'm not mad, I'm just disappointed" cut deeper than even the sharpest knife on the smoothest block of firm tofu. Human beings hate disappointing other people. It's this disappointment that pushes us to do better, be better people; to stop getting underage drinking tickets, stop running stop signs, stop dating boys that drive motorcycles and have tattoos and quit smoking cigarettes in our parents' cars.

The thing is, when it comes to disappointing ourselves, we seem to just give it a pass. Not even a second glance. Oh, you chose not to show up for your workout class that consisted of just you, your sleeping dog and a wildly, annoyingly, cheerful instructor yelling at you from the TV in your living room? Who cares if it's been months since you tied those running shoes? I can promise you this, that giant plate of nachos feels a whole heck of a lot better than your feet pounding the pavement. Just to be clear, that plate of nachos did taste a lot better than running... but that only lasted for a few minutes.

It's so easy to let ourselves down, ignore the nudges to be better and do what feels good in the moment because we do it all the time without even realizing it and our ego loves this. The disappointment isn't as clear as black spray paint on a white wall, but it's still there, staring us straight in the face. You see, when you disappoint yourself it just shows up as your physical reality.

When you don't take that job that you know you'd be fantastic for but listen to your ego go on and on about how you need more qualifications, or that woman interviewing you smiled at you funny, you just end up at a job that you totally hate and working for someone who makes your skin crawl. This is how your life shows you just how disappointed it really is. When you choose to listen to the resistance instead of learning to overcome it, you will stay stuck in whatever situation you are currently in.

Not only that, but not showing up for yourself is just one way to demolish any ounce of self-integrity you had. You see, when you show up for others but not for yourself, you're literally showing yourself that you don't even believe your own word. You are teaching yourself not to trust what you say or think and in turn, teaching yourself that your word holds no value. Because if you always say you're going to do something and then go back on it, you're not practicing self-integrity.

Doing this over and over and over again can then begin to show up in other areas of your life. Your word begins to slip when it comes to other people. You feel like what you say has no meaning or value which breaks down your self-esteem. It's a cycle and it's one that can really hurt you if you let it. How do you break the cycle? You choose to be the type of person that does exactly what you say you're going to do, especially when it comes to yourself. Doing this takes repetition and practice.

Showing up for yourself is non negotiable. Period.

Look, I've taken the easy route, ignored my own self-integrity, listened to my ego, and allowed her to control my life. I've gone down the path very well-traveled, stayed in my comfort zone and just ended up carrying around an extra 40+ pounds, living off a credit card while swimming in debt, and was left raw with a whole hell of a lot of self-loathing. If you want to change your life, start showing up for yourself whether it's convenient or not, and especially when you don't feel like it.

What do you value when it comes to your life?

That's a pretty loaded question, right? I mean you probably value lots of things but what specifically? This might not be something you think about often but next to your identity, who you believe you are and what you value is one of the leading drivers of how you show up in the world, which creates your actions and well, your physical reality.

Needless to say, values play a pretty big role but uh, if you don't know what you value, how can you stay true to those values? So, let's break down values for a second. Values simply determine what is important to you and what isn't. You can have values in any area of your life, including a romantic partner, how you make money, what you eat, even how you talk to yourself and your inner dialogue. The thing is, values are a logical thing, so your ego doesn't mind entertaining the idea of having them.

Sticking to some of them might be challenging because they may contradict the identity you've created for yourself but overall, they're easy to have. Values can be used as another filter through which you live your life, which is why they are so valuable. But they only work if you know what they are. Take a look at any area of your life that you wish was different and ask yourself; What values would you need to embody to have that area of your life change? If you're unable to think of them, remember this - polarity creates clarity. So what values *don't* you want? What's the opposite of those?

Once you have a list of values, you can create new beliefs, thoughts, and actions around those values. And as I said, values are a logic thing so your ego won't pop up as much when creating these. I'm not saying there won't be any resistance, because that's kind of your ego's forte, but there will be less. Doing this exercise is another way to create a new filter in which you create your life, instead of allowing the autopilot ego mind to do all the talking.

Writing this book was one of the biggest kicks in the lady balls for my ego. And the amount of resistance that came up was enough to make my eyes water. She tried everything to get me to give up, throw in the towel, and go back to living a life where I sat quietly in the corner. My ego tried everything from pushing me down with insults such as:

"No one will even like this book. You suck at writing and you don't even know what you're talking about. You should just give up before you make a fool of yourself. Oh yeah and the whole reason you can't think of anything to write is because you don't actually know anything about anything." [insert tongue out farting noise]

To filling my social media profiles, emails, and YouTube channels with videos of dogs having pool parties for their first birthdays. And yes, this led to me spending hours watching videos of doggos splashing around instead of sitting outside with a hot cup of coffee writing chapters.

Seriously, my ego tried everything in her power to keep me stuck and make sure I wasn't taking any action whatsoever. But you're here reading this book (I appreciate you), which means I found some way somehow to show up for myself. And not just show up but show up with the tenacity to move forward regardless of the outcome.

"Leap and the net will appear". John Burroughs.

As much as we all love this quote, the thing is, you hear it so much it becomes white noise. I mean, this saying is passed around like a fossil on show-and-tell day at school. It's one you hear, think about for a second, maybe even entertain the idea, chew on it, and then spit out and allow other, more appealing, thoughts take over your mind.

No one really wants to leap without a net. Heck, one of the most terrifying things I've ever done was leap off a 40-foot rock into an unknown depth of pitch-black water. Although to be honest, writing this book was like jumping off a 100-foot boulder into a puddle filled with snapping, snarling crocodiles.

The fact of the matter is, leaping without a net, or showing up for yourself in life, is scary. There's always a bit of hesitation or resistance. Maybe the resistance is screaming from the rooftops or maybe it's a small whisper that you can only hear for a split second. Either way, the only true way to show up for yourself is to jump into the unknown with the tenacity to keep moving forward regardless of the outcome.

If that "tweetable" sentence didn't get you jumping around taking action left and right, try this on. Whatever you believe to be true you will find evidence of because your subconscious mind is trying to prove you right. If you believe exercising is hard, getting an A in math class is impossible, or you're not smart enough to stand in front of a crowd of people and talk about your greatest passion in life, you will only see evidence of those beliefs. I'll be taking an even deeper dive into this concept in a later chapter so get your goggles ready, but for now, the point is to recognize that if you focus on the problem, that's all you will see. Cool story. You may be wondering how action actually has anything to do with all this belief and subconscious mind talk.

The thing is, action gives you solid, touch-with-your-own-hands, tangible evidence of whatever beliefs you have. Action takes you one step forward to the life you actually want to live. And guess what, once you start seeing evidence that actually supports that life, your beliefs that anything and everything is possible for you will begin to follow.

The first action you decided to take was physically picking up this book and beginning to read it. Great first step if I do say so myself! But here's a small kick in the pants; absorbing information like a sponge does nothing if you don't do something with it. So, before you even move forward - seriously, don't turn the page before you hear this- promise me and yourself that you will show up for yourself from here on out. You will take the necessary actions to live a life bigger than the bullshit your ego loves to spew. You are ready to live bigger and bolder and get uncomfortable because you know that what's on the other side is worth more than feeling discomfort for just a little while.

Say it, feel it, believe it. Now do it.

How to Show up Bigger and Bolder When Your Ego is Trying to Keep you Playing Small:

1. Ask yourself the tough questions. Questions make us feel uncomfortable because well, we're probably not going to like the answers, but asking yourself questions is imperative to showing your ego whose boss and that you mean business. Here are a few questions to start with:

- Does this action or thought align with who I want to be in life?
- What do my goals need from me?
- Who do I need to show up as to live my best life?
- Is this thought, feeling or action based in fear from my ego or from my higher self for my highest good?

2. Get comfortable with being uncomfortable. Want to know a secret? You're not growing unless you're uncomfortable. When you are uncomfortable it means you're doing something you've never done before and thus, you're out of your comfort zone. Not only that but no matter where you are in life, if you are constantly evolving and up-leveling your life, your mindset, and yourself, then something will always feel uncomfortable.

3. Use where you're going as your filter. For every single action you take, every thought you think, and feeling you feel, ask yourself, "does this align with my destination?" If it doesn't, do what you can to change that direction. Remember, your current circumstances were created by your past thoughts, feelings, and actions, which were determined by your ego.

If you want to stop your ego from controlling your life, you're going to have to take actions, feel feelings, and think thoughts that perhaps you never have before. Use your destination as your north star and follow it.

4. When you tell yourself you're going to do something, do it. Keep your word and stay true to yourself. You have to trust yourself first. Be the type of person who keeps their word. It's as simple as that.

"You have so many more answers than you think you do. You just haven't asked yourself the right questions yet."

CHAPTER 6

SHIT YOUR EGO SAYS WHEN
YOU'RE NOT LOOKING

When someone you don't really know all that well casually asks you how you're doing today, what is your knee-jerk response?

"Fine, thanks."

Or something along those lines. You just say it without even thinking because that's just the polite thing to say right? That response is basically your default response. You also have other defaults that you go back to and these defaults come in the form of the words you use when you're not thinking, the actions you take when you're in an uncomfortable situation, and ways of thinking or feeling because that's how you've always thought and felt, or that's how you were taught to think and feel, about a certain situation.

Your ego also does this when you're not paying attention. It will go back to the default thoughts, feelings, and words that are comfortable and familiar, but as you know, thinking, feeling, and saying the same things that got you here will not get you there. If you're not looking or paying attention, your ego will continue to do this and you'll just go along with it. Your ego is built to stay in the familiar. So, when you want something that is unfamiliar to you, your ego will pop in and say,

"Hey let's not do that. Let's just stay where it's safe."

By bringing up an old scenario, the old thoughts, feelings and anything else to remind you of how you've reacted to something similar in the past.

To the ego mind, unfamiliarity means possible death or harm to you. Even though what you want may be a new car, success in your businesses, or a life partner. Your ego doesn't realize the difference, it just sees familiar = safe, unfamiliar = unsafe. Which is why it will also do everything in its power to keep you stuck, stagnant, and right where you are.

My default for basically anything that I was unfamiliar with, whether it was in my business or in my personal life, was to think of an excuse why I couldn't do it, why I was better off right where I was, or to blame someone else for why it wouldn't work.

"Well, it didn't work for them, so it won't work for me."

"Oh well, that person online said it doesn't work and I shouldn't do that."

"Yeah, I should do that, or I could do that, but what if people don't like me? Or I let someone down."

I used these excuses for years. I allowed them to ruin relationships, end friendships, stir up arguments, build into massive walls of resistance and essentially, take over my life completely. Leaving me too afraid to leave the house, too afraid to put myself out there in my business and too damn afraid to show up for myself even though I knew that's what I needed and wanted to do.

The fear of the unknown and the unfamiliar will paralyze you into submission if you let it. This is why it's so crucial to recognize your ego as soon as she speaks up. Here are some common situations and ways your ego pops your bubble and speaks up in your life.

"What if you become so successful everyone leaves you or thinks you're stuck up?"

You then sabotage your way through life to ensure you will not be successful so you won't have to deal with losing the people you love.

"If you show up on that live video everyone will make fun of you."

You stop showing up in your business and it doesn't grow.

"Loving yourself too much means you're cocky and nobody wants to date someone like that."

You continue to put yourself down and only attract unfavorable people that either make you feel worse or are just as brutal to themselves.

"Starting that blog or podcast is stupid. There are so many other people doing exactly what you want to do so just let them do it instead of you."

"I'll just stay quiet because if I speak up people will start looking at me. And if people start listening to me then I have to say all the right things. And if I don't say the right things then people will hate me." OR, "I have to be the loudest person in the room, because if I'm not the center of attention and people aren't looking at me then they're forgetting about me and if I'm forgotten I'll be alone forever."

Have you ever noticed how the people who are the loudest in the room, the center of attention, or the biggest bully on the playground are always the most insecure? It's because they are living by their default mindset and just doing what is familiar to them. Chances are, they are also living in fear based on what happened in the past. The fear of not being heard and forgotten about then possibly ending up alone, or the fear of not getting the attention and the validation that they need to know what kind of person they are. Even the fear of being left out, or FOMO as the kids call it these days. It's all doused in fear and based on the past.

These are the default thoughts put into your mind via your past experiences, what people have told you, society, among other things and because they are familiar to you, you are more likely to listen to them than go against the grain and think something else. Most of these thoughts and words come to you as your excuses for why you should or shouldn't do something. This is why I have an entire chapter on showing up for yourself, because if you don't, your ego will take over in any way she possibly can.

Here's the thing, life doesn't necessarily change when you're all excited for the five minutes it takes to mediate, exercise, eat a salad, or read a really insightful post on social media. The changes come long after the excitement wears off and you're less than enthused about your refrigerator filled with greens, you're sick of that annoying little reminder that always pops up on your phone about a meditation you said you'd do, and you begin looking for celebrity gossip when you become bored of insightful posts on social media.

Life changes when everything goes back to normal and your defaults start to set in but you make the conscious decision to continue to make changes regardless. If you want to get very clear on your default thoughts, words, and behaviors, take a look at your habits.

If you have a habit of always saying no when a friend asks you out for coffee because you're afraid of what people will think of you when you leave the house, that friend will eventually stop asking you out for coffee and will probably fall out of your life completely. When you let your default habits created by your ego dictate your life, you miss out on opportunities that could propel you forward. You miss out on the people, places and things that just may have the answers you're so desperately searching for.

Lies Your Ego Tells You to Keep You Safe:

- "I'm not ready yet!"
- "I need something outside of myself to be happy."
- "I have to change who I am to fit in."
- "My self-worth is determined by how much other people like me."
- "It's everyone else's fault that I am the way I am."
- "You'll bother them if you ask for help."
- "I don't have time."
- "I can't."
- "I don't deserve it."
- "I just don't have what it takes."
- "I'll just do it tomorrow instead."
- "I don't know."
- "I'm not responsible."
- "Everything wrong in life is happening to me."
- "I'm not lucky."

- "I have to do more."
- "I can't have it/do it/be it, because..."
- "I am the way I am because..."
- "If people don't like me then I'm just not worthy of love."

Have you ever found yourself saying these things out loud or in your head? Chances are, you have. We all have at one point or another. But without breaking all these lies down and throwing them back in your egos face, I want you to take note of the commonalities. Your ego doesn't like to take responsibility, and throws it out onto someone else. Your ego acts out of fear and makes rash decisions. Your ego believes you need something outside of yourself in order to get whatever it is you want. Your ego likes to pretend it has a poker face, like a stone-cold wall, but in reality, it has tells. Massive ones. You just have to be willing to look through a different lens to see them.

Your ego also loves to over generalize by using words like: "everyone", "always", "every single time", etc. Your ego loves to spew these lies on a daily basis and they often happen without you even noticing. Which is why it is so important to create a pattern interrupt in your thinking. The point is to become aware of the thoughts, words, and beliefs that roll around inside your head on a daily basis. You won't be able to grab a hold of all of them, but if you can snatch some of them up you can look them in the eye and decide for yourself if they are true or not. Remember, your ego is like a child. If you don't want the child version of yourself driving your car, take back the wheel by taking back your thoughts and stories that form around them.

The Tipping Point

If you had all your daily thoughts sitting on a seesaw, 50% thoughts that help you on one side and 50% thoughts that hurt you on the other side, all it takes to make a change and create a tipping point is to add one more percent to the thoughts that are helping you. That's it. 51%. In practical terms this means about 13 hours of your day are put towards the thoughts, feelings, and stories that help you change your life. Maybe that seems like a lot, maybe it doesn't.

The point is to become aware; become aware that it doesn't take that much time to switch your thoughts, and it doesn't require you to be 100% all of the time. Only 51% and you've created a tipping point of change. In other words, think about it like this - if you can think about all the things that could go wrong, you can also think about all the things that can go right. Choose to switch your thoughts from what could go wrong, to daydreaming about what could go right. The time is going to pass anyway. Why not rig it in your favor?

How to Create a Pattern Interrupt:

Pattern interrupts are used to interrupt certain behaviors, thoughts, and actions or really just get you used to throwing a wrench into your default thinking and start moving the gears a different way.

1. **Question everything.** You're going to begin to notice that throughout this book I ask a lot of questions. Why? Because as Richard Bandler said, "The quality of your life is determined by the quality of the questions you ask."

   If you want to kick your ego to the back seat of your life, you need to start questioning everything. For every action you take, thought you think, and feeling you have, question it.

   "Really? *No one* likes me?"

   "Has there ever been a time when I didn't feel ready but did it anyway?"

   "Does this make sense?"

   "Can I choose to put my focus on something that makes me feel more empowered?"

   Seriously, get really good at questioning yourself and your mind will have no choice but to find you answers and they're going to be answers that your ego probably isn't going to like.

2. **Do something out of your routine.** Routines are great and necessary but as a human being, evolving and growing all the time, you may be forgetting to expand your routine to match where you are in life. Start changing it up, walking a different way, driving a different way to work, listening to something else, mediating at night instead of the morning, whatever. Change up your routine and you'd be surprised at what else can change in your life.

3. **Awareness is key.** 95% of people go through life on autopilot. The ego mind LOVES this. Being aware of what you are doing, what you are thinking, and what you are feeling and what triggered that response is imperative to tossing out your old ego-based thoughts, actions, and feelings.

   Become aware of when your ego gets the loudest, take note of the thoughts that come up throughout the day and understand if they were ego-based thoughts (fear based) or higher self-based (moving you forward). This takes practice but starting now is the perfect place to start.

"Your ego and the people around you like to wrap their fear in 'I'm just doing/saying this because I want to keep you safe' wrapping paper and slap a bow on top. So, we believe them and avoid taking any action at all."

CHAPTER 7

SELF-LOVE IS YOUR EGO'S NEMESIS

The story of self-love and your ego is basically the best protagonist vs antagonist movie never made. Self-love of course being the hero that saves everybody and your ego being the highly misunderstood villain that learns a very valuable lesson in the end. Needless to say, if you want to stop your ego cold in its self-deprecating tracks, throw some love at it. You see, self-love is like everything but the bagel seasoning - you can put that shit on everything and it makes your life 10x as amazing.

Loving yourself fully and completely is the one thing your ego cannot compete with because your ego only makes decisions based on fear. Throwing love at the fear quiets your ego, calms your mind, and allows your higher self to step in and call the shots for once. But why does love work so well when it comes to putting the kibosh on your ego mind?

Simply put, love is blind. When you put your heart shaped love goggles on, nothing, and I mean nothing, can stop you. Think about it; when you first fall in love with another person it's like the whole world just falls away and it's just you and them as far as your eye can see. And if anyone has anything different to say about your love story, you just tune them out and skip and summersault all the way back to your love bubble. So why can't you fall in love with yourself so much outside influences fall away?

Because all your life you were trained not to. But you're also trained to. To be honest, society, your parents, the people that raised you and the people you looked up to as well, as the people you spend the most time with, all tell you contradicting stories. As children we're told we can grow up to be anything we want to be. If you're lucky. Really?? I get to be a doctor or an astronaut or live in a sanctuary with all my animal friends?? And then as you get older and tell your adult friends and family you're quitting your dusty old 9-5 job to officially chase your dreams and become a full-time blogger, a YouTuber, or even build that sanctuary you've always wanted, boom, just like that you're dodging their fears and criticisms about what could go wrong instead of basking in the glow of compliments and woo hoos for actually goin' for it. Why? Because you're an adult now and you have to be "realistic". Whatever that means. You are told you should love yourself and go for your dreams, but not too much and to always have a backup plan for when it doesn't work out, and to not be self- centered and take too many selfies because then you'll look like you're too in love yourself. This is the world we live in, where everyone has a contradicting opinion and are so consumed by what the people are doing next to them, they forget the whole point of life is to live it.

This is why loving yourself comes in so handy. Because when you love yourself and truly mean it, you slap on your love googles and the rest of the world's opinions fall away and it's just you, your heart, and your dreams livin' it up. But what do you do if you don't know how to love yourself? Like where do you even begin?

Remember back to when you were a child. Living wild and free. Ripping off your clothes and running around the neighborhood buck naked for everyone to see without a care in the world. Or peeing your pants and kissing toads in front of your older brother's friends just because they told you to and you couldn't care less what they thought about you.

Children live, laugh, and "be" without a care in the world. Why? Because they unconditionally love themselves and have yet to be taught otherwise. They know nothing about body image, that you "should" be embarrassed about your stretch marks, or you "should" tone yourself down for others, or it's not okay to cry if you're hurting. These are behaviors and beliefs that are taught to you by the people you grow up with. And the ego takes these beliefs and stories and wraps them up in meanings about who you are as a person. Which makes you believe you are not worthy of love, or acceptance. That you have to be a certain way to fit in or that there is something wrong with you if you don't fit into a certain box.

When you practice self-love, your ego loses her ability to control you and put you down. She can jabber on all she wants but you're too busy scribbling your own name in your notebook and uh, ya know, living your best damn life to even care. Oh, and if you're worried about coming across as conceited, vain or just too "into yourself", that's not what this chapter, or self-love, is about. And by the way, that's just your ego talking out of fear that you might actually fall in love with the person you are and start listening to your heart over her. If you want to live a bigger life, I suggest dropping that notion off and leaving it in this chapter. You don't need it anymore.

The act of self-love comes in many different forms and affirmations, like looking at yourself naked in the mirror, or taking the necessary time off to rejuvenate, or exercise, and don't worry, I'll get into all that but first, I want to talk about a sneaky way the ego likes to show up in our lives when things with ourselves are just starting to get serious. Your ego begins to look to others to validate what you are doing, the actions you are taking, if you're on the right path, and if you're liked and accepted. But, not only does your ego look to others to validate your thoughts and feelings and what you are doing to make sure you are "fitting in" and are "normal" compared to everyone else, your ego also likes to use other people to evaluate where you should be based on where those other people currently are. Similar to a ranking system to show you who's on top and who's not. This is a very primal instinct to show you if your spot in the tribe is threatened or not. Of course, you no longer have a "tribe" per se but stick with me here.

When you scroll on social media or watch television and see people who are successful or doing "better" than you who have circumstances that contradict what you believe, such as, if you believe that you have to have a famous parent to be famous, or access to certain things and lots of money to be successful, and then you see a successful person who contradicts those beliefs, such as they grew up poor, or didn't have access to the internet or whatever the case may be; you begin to compare your life to theirs and measure yourself against them. If you feel you don't measure up it makes you feel angry, upset, and downright horrible and then, because your ego simply cannot be wrong, you start to make excuses for why you are where you are and why they are where they are. This is also when your ego tries to devalue what they have done to bring them back down to your level. Because if they're back down to your level then you're not wrong anymore.

Comparison is a trap that will swallow you whole if you let it. You could spend hours, weeks, even months or years comparing where you are to where someone else is. But let me ask you this. Has comparing yourself to someone else ever helped you move forward with your dreams? Has taking a magnifying glass to your life and someone else's actually gotten you further? I'm going to take a guess here and say a resounding no.

Look, I could sit here all day and give you a million and one reasons not to compare yourself to others, and then give you another million ways to stop. At the end of the day all that matters is where you are, where you're going, and the fun, exciting, messy bits in the middle. You need to decide that moving forward is more important to you than standing still and looking at someone else's life while your own passes you by. Focus on the outcome, but be grateful for the journey. As tough as it may be to call yourself out and take a look at what you are saying about yourself, it's also imperative to notice what you are saying about other people. Because what you are saying about others tells you a lot about what you are feeling about yourself. And this need and immense burning for external validation, or the feeling and belief that there's not enough to go around for all of us, can be one of the most crippling feelings in the world.

There was a time when I felt I wasn't getting the validation I needed or deserved from someone in my life and I sure as all hell wasn't giving it to myself, so I went searching for it from other people. I used men to tell me if I was "good" enough, pretty enough, worthy enough, of life and when they made me feel like I wasn't, I changed myself for them. You want a nice quiet girl? No problem. You want a girl with blonde hair that wears tight clothes only when you're around? You got it. You want a girl that keeps her mouth shut? Done.

The thing is, I didn't just do this around men, I changed my entire personality to fit anyone I chose to spend my time with. Why? Because I just wanted their approval. I wanted to be liked, loved, adored. I wanted to be the funniest person in the room, the best-looking person in the room, the only girl they were talking to or looking at. And when I didn't get that I sabotaged the relationship and blamed it on them. I was so quick to change for someone else at the drop of a hat. But when it came to changing for myself to get the life I wanted, I stood cold in my tracks. Why? Because I believed those people, those external sources, would give me the love and validation I was so desperately seeking. I was so blinded by that thought and belief that I could only be as good as what someone said about me that I didn't even realize that what I was looking for was right in front of my face the entire time.

That's what self-love does for you. Self-love gives you the validation that you didn't receive from someone you loved, it gives you the permission to live bigger, bolder, more loudly, and it allows you to show up in all your glittery, glowing glory in life. Self-love also gives you the necessary nudge to take action. Okay, it basically pushes you out of the plane with a giant heart shaped parachute. When you love yourself just as you are so blindingly, you check that the parachute is tied tight and take the leap knowing and believing that even if you run into some turbulence along the way, it'll only make you stronger.

A Hard Lesson on Gossip

Raise your hand if you've ever said anything mean about someone else. I raised my hand too. It happens. But here's something you need to know. Your subconscious mind takes everything personally. Yeah, so when you say something negative about someone else, your subconscious thinks you are talking about yourself. If you truly want to work on your self-love muscle, start throwing that love at other people too because it's going to come back to you as well.

Self-love Takes Practice

How do you really practice self-love so it sticks, stop seeking validation from others, and tell your ego to pack a bag and get outta here? Just like a muscle in the body, in order for your self-love muscle to get stronger, you have to work on it every single day. The more you practice, the stronger it will get and the easier it will become to love yourself unconditionally.

How to Love Yourself Unconditionally

1. **Watch your words.** The words we say about ourselves are the biggest tell of how we feel, which then shows us how we're going to show up in the world. Let me be the first to tell you that the mean girl inside your head is just your ego trying to keep you right where you are.

If you find yourself strolling past a mirror and your immediate thought is, "why am I so fat and unattractive? No one could ever love me", these words will then become your truth and that is what you will begin to believe.

Instead, practice saying three things you love about yourself. You can start with your personality first if you find that easier and then work your way to your physical self.

   a) Practice affirmations on a daily basis. Affirmations are simply words or phrases usually said as "I am" statements used to create new beliefs and evoke empowering feelings. I know, I know, you might be rolling your eyes at this one but affirmations are an extremely powerful way to reprogram your subconscious and when said enough on a consistent basis, you begin to believe them.

Start by looking yourself in the mirror or standing up with your hands on your hips and saying:

"I am an incredible person", "I am valuable", "I am worthy"

Choose "I am" statements that make YOU feel powerful, excited, and damn good about yourself!

2. **Celebrate your wins!** My favorite analogy is this; life is like climbing up a mountain, and most of the time we are so focused on how far we have left to go, we forget how far we've

actually come. So, when you're climbing up that mountain of life, look back just long enough to pat yourself on the back for how far you've come.

3. **Spend time doing things that make you FEEL good.** Really simple but you'd be surprised how often we forget to do this.

4. **Forgive yourself.** One of the most detrimental things our egos can do is replay our past faults over and over and over again until they consume us. Whatever was done in the past is done and the best way to correct it is to do better today than you did yesterday. Forgive yourself for making mistakes, forgive yourself for feeling, and let go of thoughts that are not helping you move forward.

I could go on but we need to get a move on with the next chapter so the point is, love your dang self like your life depends on it...because it does.

"Once you finally give yourself the validation you've been craving, you will no longer seek it from the world."

CHAPTER 8

GREAT ANSWERS COME FROM GREAT QUESTIONS

Sometimes the life you've been wanting to live is quietly crawling in the grass just waiting for the perfect time to strike. Or in my case, biting me in the ass while I was just minding my own business, having a perfectly lovely picnic in my backyard with my dog. I do that a lot but that's beside the point. When I started this whole overcoming my ego and deciding to live a bigger life thing, I made the decision to rid myself and my mind of negativity. I also made the conscious decision to stop blaming the world for my problems. And as someone who walked down the street with a chip on their shoulder bigger than Mt. Everest, this proved to be a bigger challenge than I could have ever imagined.

This challenge began with ridding my mind of negativity. Which meant changing and controlling the things I could in my environment, like not watching the news, removing people on social media that were not serving who I wanted to be, ending friendships that weren't healthy for me, you know, the whole nine. Well, my ego was having none of that and immediately started bringing everything that I was trying to release to my attention. People around me that didn't normally talk about the sometimes extremely dark world we live in started telling me horrible stories about the world around me, my social media accounts once again filled up with anger, arguments, and complaints and I found nit-picky reasons to be angry and of course, "none of it was my fault". Blaming my external circumstances felt good. It felt real and for even just a little bit, it took the pain away.

I can remember sitting in this pit of destruction for days until one day while having a picnic in my backyard, something crawled into my sweatpants and bit me in the ass. Literally. Although I don't actually know what it was that bit me, it startled me so much that it actually drove me out of my depth of despair. And instead of sitting in these feelings and allowing my ego to take control I started questioning everything that my ego was trying to bring up. I started poking holes in the legitimacy of the stories I was telling myself and this stirred up one of the most valuable lessons I've ever learned.

Learning to objectively ask yourself result-based questions is one of the most crucial ways to change your life, get out of your head, and out of your own way. Asking yourself these types of questions is also one of the easiest ways to tell your ego to fluff off and let her know that you're here ready to live a bigger and bolder life thank you very much. Here's the thing though, your ego likes to ask you questions too, but they're usually not very helpful and you guessed it, end up leaving you stuck in the same exact place.

"Why is this happening to me?"

"What did I do to deserve this?"

"Why does everything bad have to happen to me?"

These types of questions keep you focused on the problem and don't allow you to find a solution. Which just keeps making you feel well, even more stuck and when you think you're stuck you are programming your subconscious mind to continually find more evidence of that. And when you keep asking yourself questions that keep you stuck, you eventually stop moving forward or anywhere at all. Not only that but "why" based questions give your ego reasons to dig her claws even deeper into why your life looks the way it looks. Opening the door for her to make even more excuses that are harder to get rid of than they were before.

This is why learning to interrupt your pattern of thinking with new result-based questions is so powerful. Not only can result-based questions get you out of your head but they can help stop the very powerful cloud of circling thoughts and worries that the ego likes to yell inside your head.

Result-based questions are like this:

"What can I do right now to find the answer I am looking for?"

"What internal resources do I have to help me find the answer that I am looking for?"

"What is this undesirable situation trying to teach me?"

"I'm having this feeling. What do I want to feel instead of this? What is the opposite feeling?"

"What can I do differently to get the result I desire?"

Asking yourself questions like these help you get out of your own box of thinking and once you're out of the box, you're able to see the solution that you simply couldn't see while sitting inside the box. Result-based questions are questions that allow you to see the problem or unwanted situation just long enough to see a solution, or at least look for a solution. Which gives your subconscious mind a chance to search for one. And when your subconscious mind is busy doing its job (making sure you're right), your ego has no opportunity to run you ragged with unhelpful thoughts and worries. Remember, your subconscious mind is like a computer running whatever program you give it, so give it a good one.

This whole process of switching your own questioning around might sound really simple, and it is, but it's not always the easiest thing in the world to do. When a problem, unwanted situation, or outcome arises, the first initial thought is to blame it on something external. That's what your ego is good at. It's easy. It doesn't take as much effort and most importantly, it doesn't cause any pain or discomfort.

External problems are also the easiest thing to grab for. They're the first place you look to find evidence of your problem. Oh, this person did this and that is why I feel angry, or it's the phone companies' fault for marketing their phones as waterproof when they're just water resistant. Think of it like swimming in the ocean. If you flail around trying to stay afloat you'll lose all your energy very quickly and your initial instinct will be to grab for something, anything solid to keep you up and out of the water, but if you just let go and allow yourself to be still, you will float.

The hard route is to call yourself out. Ask yourself the tough questions. Lean into the discomfort, lean into the pain, and be open to figuring it out. This lesson will come up again and again and again in life and the only way to truly get this down is to make it a habit. Make it a habit of calling yourself out and asking the uncomfortable questions. Make it a habit of leaning in and asking questions that give you a real answer. Just like a muscle that needs to be worked out consistently to stay strong, your question muscle has to stay strong as well.

You may be wondering how you can even tell if you're asking yourself the right questions or not. And the easiest way to figure that out is if you ask yourself a question and you're still "stuck" in the problem. If you're driving in a car and come up on some roadwork and you ask yourself problem-based questions such as:

"Why is this happening?"

"Why in the actual BLEEP would they be doing roadwork at this time of night."

Is your car going to move anywhere? Are you any closer to your destination now after asking those questions? No? Okay try again. And this time ask yourself questions that will help keep you moving forward. It's when you become willing to look for an answer, even an answer you may not want to hear, that you'll find it. For a clearer example of questions from the ego vs questions from your higher self/intuition, refer back to the chart in chapter 3.

Another simple way to ensure you are asking the best questions possible is to make sure you are focusing on "what" questions instead of "why" questions. "Why" questions focus on reasons and excuses which are usually things you have no control over because they are external. "What" based questions force you to look internally, allowing your subconscious to do what it does best and pop out an answer that will give you results. Your ego will always look for reasons why, your higher self will always look for ways you can be at cause.

I Don't Know.

For years I had this habit of saying, "I don't know." But I wouldn't say it just once, oh no, I would say it multiple times just to reiterate how much I really didn't know. I would say it for everything. Literally. Big questions, small questions, all of them. I said "I don't know" so often that it became my default response. Whether I knew the answer or not, that was the first thing that came out of my mouth. Doing so gave my ego all the time in the world to play games inside my head and come up with all the little things that I "didn't know".

I'm not one for absolutes, but if you can eliminate one phrase from your internal and external dialogue, get rid of this one; "I don't know" takes away all of your power. It's like taking away the keyboard and shutting off the search results for your subconscious mind. And because your words and thoughts are just a self-fulfilling prophecy, what do you think you'll see more evidence of? Not knowing.

Now I'm not saying that you should just know the answer right away or become someone who is considered a "know-it-all". What I am saying is choose a different language pattern. One that can actually help you find the answer instead of one that leaves you scratching your head. Try this on for size, "I'm searching for the answer right now." Or, "I know the answer is coming to me now." Or even, "If I did know the answer it would be x, y, z." Give your subconscious something to grab onto with a direct command. Trust me, you know a lot more than you think you do. You just have to allow your mind to do the work for you.

I know.

I know I shouldn't date men that hurt me.

I know I should exercise for my health.

I know I should put that bottle of wine down and stop drinking.

I know, I know, I know!

Do you really "know" something if you haven't experienced it yet and gotten the result you wanted?

Does "knowing" something automatically mean you get the outcome you want?

Has saying "I know" ever given you the answer you were looking for?

I talked about "I don't know" so I thought it was only fitting to also talk about the opposite response. Which I've had first-hand experience with, also throwing it at anything and everything I could. These might be some of the most frustrating questions you ask yourself. But that's what this book is about, making you think. Pushing you out of your box and asking you questions that require you to look outside of your own box to find the answers. The next time you notice yourself saying "I know" or "I don't know", stop and think about if those responses will give you the result you're looking for and if not, try something else.

If you're truly committed to calling yourself out and asking yourself the right questions here are practical ways to strengthen your "question muscle":

1. As soon as an unwanted outcome or situation comes up, recognize where your mind goes and get present to the questions that immediately come up. If these questions are not giving you answers but instead leaving you with more and more and more questions, get quiet, take three deep breaths and try again.

2. Start asking yourself result-based questions or questions that can give you real tangible evidence of a solution to the problem. These questions will give your subconscious mind a job and will allow you to become more present to the solution.

3. Practice asking yourself these types of questions for everything. The more you practice, the easier this will become.

4. Try catching yourself in the act of saying "I don't know" when you don't know something and instead try on different phrases that will help you search for the answer. Remember, your subconscious is like a computer that is always on, always listening, and always giving you exactly what you ask for. Also choose to catch yourself in the opposite, "I know". Chances are, most of these answers are not giving you the result you're looking for and are leaving you spinning your wheels even more than you were before.

"One of the most valuable lessons you can learn is to objectively ask yourself result-based questions. Even if you're afraid of the answer."

CHAPTER 9

I won't be happy until...

One of the greatest and most painful tricks of your ego mind is that she will have you believe that if you change everything on the outside, then and only then will you feel whatever it is you are searching to feel. If you have x, you will be a completely different person and then things will be different. If you have y, then you'll be happy or confident, if you have z, then life will be easy and fun. If only I had a super cute, hot, sexy boyfriend, then I would be happy and I would show up differently in the world. If I could only lose 50 pounds then I would be happier and I would gain all this confidence and would finally be the confident person I've always wanted to be. If I had the house, the car, the family, the vacation home then I'd be different. Then I would be happy. This is how you're taught to think. If you have something, you will take a different action which will make you a different person or at least show up differently. This is also what I like to call the happiness fallacy. You believe that if you have something external it will change who you are on the inside, which is simply not true, but your ego believes it is because again, it's the easy route.

So, you go out there and you chase after all these external things expecting them to change how you feel, how you think. Expecting them to make you happy. Finally. And when that doesn't work it feels like you've failed. Like you've tried everything but you still feel the same way - you don't feel any better, you just have a different external circumstance. But, what the hell? Why don't you feel like a completely different person? Why aren't you happy? So, you go out there and do it again and again and again and again while getting the same results, again and again and again. What keeps happening is all you've changed is the external part of you while the way you think, your beliefs, your habits, and your feelings all remain the same.

This is why when people lose weight without addressing why they gained weight in the first place or the mental health side of weight loss, they gain it back. They didn't get what they wanted out of it. This is why when I chased men to fill something and make me feel whole and complete, I still felt lost and miserable. Which led me to chase other external things that had made me feel "good" in the past, such as food and alcohol. None of these things worked in making me feel happy, loved, or validated because I had to give myself those things by changing who I was being on the inside.

Why do you chase after these things if they won't make you feel the happiness, the pleasure, the validation, whatever you want to feel? Because our ego is looking for something, anything to feel good in the moment. A quick fix. That instant gratification. What will give me validation right here and now? What will fill me up? What will make me feel happy even if it's fleeting? Doing the inner work isn't quick, it isn't glamorous or sexy and it doesn't give you what you're looking for immediately. But from a young age you are taught, or more accurately your brain is hammered from day one, with the idea that if you have this external thing, then you will be happy. You are taught to focus on something outside of yourself to bring you joy and happiness.

The cold hard truth is, if you weren't happy without it, you won't be happy with it.

Think about it like this; if you put a scalding hot cup of coffee into a thermos that is built to keep things hot and then you douse that thermos with water from the Arctic Ocean (the coldest ocean in the world according to Google), do you think once you open that thermos the coffee has changed into an iced mocha latte? No, because all that was changed was an external state. It was put into cold water but the inside stayed hot and until you add some ice cubes to the scalding hot cup of coffee it won't change. The point is, unless you change your thoughts, feelings, perspectives, and actions on the inside, you can change your outside all you want but it won't bring you the internal change you desire.

You might be rolling your eyes at me right now and thinking something along the lines of, "yeah freaking right." If I had everything I wanted, the money, the car, the house, the sexy significant other, the body of my dreams, of course I'd be happy! Okay I'll bite. Let's just say that yeah, you got everything you ever wanted and then you felt happy for a while but eventually you feel this urge for more. A feeling like you're lacking something that can only be fixed by someone or something else. So, you start chasing after something new. And then you want more so you chase after another external thing and then another and then another.

Then after a while or even right away, your ego begins to attach your identity to the objects or people you've brought into your life.

Your ego starts to identify you based on what you have or don't have. So, you start questioning who you would be without these things. Then your ego starts to fear losing these things because to your ego, losing your identity is detrimental to your safety. And those things you wanted no longer make you happy because you're too busy being afraid of losing them. And what you focus on you just create more of. Fear, lack, worry. They all expand like a sponge when you give them water or in this case, attention and focus. Simply put, if you want to be happy, create it in your mind first.

By now you already know your ego is pretty sneaky, attaching to fear to keep you safe and hell bent on keeping you in your comfort zone. Your ego also loves to attach your identity to your external circumstances as a way to help you figure out where you stand in the world. And if you've been paying attention, you already know that you have the power to change your external reality based on where you put your attention and your own personal perspective and that if you kick your ego into the back seat and allow your higher self to take the wheel, life will be a hell of a lot more fun. This means that without fail, you can choose where you put your attention right here, right now. You can choose to feel the feelings you think those external things will give you.

I'll let you in on a little secret - allowing yourself to feel amazing, joyful, excited, whatever you want to feel now, without anything or anyone in control of those feelings (besides your mind of course), is one of the most freeing feelings in the world. And knowing that you don't "need" anything to make you happy or feel fulfilled is indescribable. It's also just another way to tell your ego to fluff off and allow your higher self to enjoy the scenery for once. Living your life and allowing your happiness to be added or taken away by circumstances you can't control is like baking a pie, setting it out in the sun and then getting mad when it rots. You cannot control the sun, you cannot control other people, you cannot control your external circumstances, but you can control how you decide to feel.

But don't get it twisted, having all the things you want in life just makes life that much more fun, I mean that's what we were meant to come here and do. And no, it's not selfish to want things or to have everything you want. That's just your ego talking. Being happy now is like having a delicious double chocolate, cookie dough surprise cupcake with vanilla icing. All the things you want: the car, the house, the boyfriend or girlfriend, the 50 dogs, etc. are the sprinkles on top. No matter how you look at it, you still get to enjoy a damn good cupcake! But instead of worrying if someone is going to take it away from you, you've created your own recipe for happiness which means you can whip it up any time you want.

I know you're wondering how you're supposed to feel happy right here right now without having all the external things you desire.

First, ask yourself these questions:

What do I want "x" (the external person, place or thing you want) to make me feel?

Do I have all the internal resources I need to feel this way now?

Who can I be right now to feel these feelings that I am looking for?

Get very clear on these questions to help you really understand the exact feelings you are wanting to feel. As soon as you ask yourself these questions, your subconscious mind will get to work on finding the answer, so be ready.

Next, do the things that will help you feel those feelings now. Pretty simple right? But if you can't think of anything right now, start by moving your body. Emotion means energy in motion so if you want to move stagnant energy around (usually these are feelings that don't feel very good) start by simply moving. You can also immediately shift your perspective by thinking about something that does make you happy and feel good. Your happiness is in your hands.

Ways to Feel Good Feelings Now

Affirmation: I am becoming someone who creates their own joy and happiness now.

5. **Get outside in nature.** Nature is the most abundant thing on the planet, and just sitting in it can help you feel grounded and immediately lift your mood. You can even take off your shoes and walk through the grass or hug a tree, whatever floats your boat.

6. **Crank up your favorite music.** As I said, emotion means energy in motion and moving your body is one of the best ways to move out old, stagnant energy. So, get up and cut a rug!

7. **Find three things you're grateful for and write them down.** Gratitude is one of the easiest ways to see the good in your life and will automatically make you feel good. You can also turn this into a daily morning practice if you would like.

8. **Treat yourself.** Take yourself out to dinner and a movie. Get your bubble bath on. Have a spa day. Do whatever makes you feel good and remember to love your dang self!

9. **Hold the door for someone, say thank you, smile at a stranger.** Doing something nice for someone else can immediately boost your mood and it doesn't cost a thing.

"Exchanging one external thing for another external thing will not solve your internal problems."

CHAPTER 10

FEAR IS THE FUEL TO YOUR EGO'S STORIES

Fear is like the giant purple elephant in the room. You can see it, you can hear it, you can smell it but you don't talk about it because it's scary to talk about. See the irony there? But since you've read this far, I'm sure you've noticed a theme; your ego is based in fear. Doused in it is more accurate. Fear is the literal fuel to your ego's stories. Without fear, your ego doesn't survive. As I've said, we need the ego and "fear" to keep us out of life-threatening situations, which your brain is fantastic at doing, so this chapter is not about getting rid of the fear or ignoring it and pretending it'll just go away. This is about facing the fear that's keeping you stuck head on, giant white tusks and all, and doing what you know you need to do regardless of the fear that you feel. But before you can begin to dismantle the fears and charge through them, you need to understand what fear actually is and how the ego likes to present it to you, because yes, fear comes in all different shapes and sizes and it's always wrapped up in different colored wrapping paper with a bow on top. Making it appear different on the outside when on the inside it all comes from the same place.

First of all, what actually is fear? Well, fear is a biological and emotional response induced by a perceived threat. You know the feeling. You walk out onto a stage and overlook a crowded room of 100 people and you can hear your heart pounding in your ears. You walk into your garage and see the biggest freaking spider you've ever seen and run away screaming. You walk down a dark alleyway at night and look around while picking up your pace. Or maybe, you look at your bank account and feel the urge to curl into a ball of despair.

These fears come from two places; one being your subconscious programming, the other a more primal, survival state. The difference between your subconscious programming fear and your survival fear is that your subconsciously programmed fear can be changed just as easily as it was programmed. The other survival fear will always be there to keep you alive. This type of fear will never go away because it is necessary for your survival. So, don't worry about getting rid of your fears, your mind will always know what to do when you are in a truly life-threatening situation. Your focus for this chapter is the fear that keeps you playing small and in your comfort zone.

Fear manifests itself in many different ways including: the fear of rejection, the fear of success, the fear of failure, the fear of judgment, and FOMO (fear of missing out). This doesn't even scratch the surface. Although fear shows up in your life in a plethora of ways, it's all coming from the same thing; the fear of what that thing/event means about who you are. The fear is created by the meaning you give it about who you are as a person.

Let's look at the fear of failure for example. If you are afraid of failure it is because you are afraid of what that means about you on an identity level. If I fail, then that means I am [fill in the blank]. This story was created as a child by someone else. Maybe a parent or relative, sibling or any trusted adult. And your ego latches onto your identity for dear life because your identity is familiar so anything that threatens your identity, or does not confirm your identity, will be distorted to fit into the box that your ego creates to make sure it aligns with who you are.

Meaning, if you're afraid to fail because you were taught it means you are not good enough, you become someone who is afraid to fail and then you take subconscious actions that align with that identity. Not only that, but you may also subconsciously self-sabotage any action that could possibly take you out of your comfort zone. And this is all simply based on the fear-based meaning you gave failure.

You may now be thinking that fear is bad and you should avoid it at all costs and just not feel fear ever again. Well I choose to see it differently. Fear is neither good nor bad, it just *is*. Fear teaches you lessons; it keeps you safe in life threatening situations and it teaches you where you need to learn and grow. Once you change the meaning of fear, it immediately loses its power.

So, how is this whole subconscious fear created and programmed, if it's subconscious? Well, it was created by our parents and guardians when we were kids. If your parents acted fearful around money, saying things like,

"Money doesn't grow on trees."

"We can't afford that."

"Only buy what you need and nothing more."

"Don't spoil yourself too much."

Your subconscious mind took in the words and feelings of your parents and turned them into beliefs. And because your subconscious beliefs create your actions, these words and fears simply turned into a self-fulfilling prophecy. Meaning, whatever you believe to be true you see evidence of in your physical reality. These stories also became familiar, making them pop up over and over and over again.

This subconscious programming continues throughout your whole life, until you decide to consciously change it. It's like a computer program that's simply doing its job. And until you put in a new program, it will continue to work the way it's supposed to work. Don't worry though, reprogramming your subconscious mind and beliefs are something we will dive into in upcoming chapters but for now I want to focus on how to overcome the fear and see it for what it truly is.

The first thing to understand is that unless you are in a life-threatening situation, the fear you're feeling is just an illusion of the ego mind. Your ego is pulling in thoughts that create emotions about a particular thing and it does this to make sure you are staying in familiar situations and aligning your behavior with your habits. Because familiarity means you're safe, at least according to your ego mind. As soon as you decide that what you're doing is no longer scary anymore and simply change the meaning of the fear, you no longer see it as something to avoid.

Chances are, the fear is there because of a story you created around what the fear means. If you're afraid to do something ask yourself; What about doing that thing is scary? And remember, at the end of the day, you get to decide what fear means to you. All you have to do to create a new story is to notice when fear comes up, ask yourself if this fear is serving you or hurting you, then create a new narrative that better suits you by reframing the fear.

I am scared to do Facebook Lives —-> This emotion of fear that I am feeling around Facebook Lives is exciting because it means I'm stepping out of my comfort zone and doing something that I've never done before, which means I'm growing!

I'm too afraid to do x, y, z because people will laugh at me —-> I choose to believe in myself and realize that what other people do or say is a reflection of them, not me.

Here's another trick to remember; what you focus on amplifies. Think about a time when you were lying in bed trying to drift off to sleep but you kept going over and over in your head about your big meeting coming up, or that book you had to write, or whatever it is that brings up fear and worry within you, and the more you thought it about the more afraid and worried you got? This is because whatever you focus on amplifies. One way to reduce these fears and feeling like there is a tiny hamster running on a wheel inside your head is to focus on the here and now. This very moment. Are you safe? Are you taken care of? Bringing your focus into the present moment will immediately remove you from the thoughts of the future. Another trick is to reframe those thoughts by asking yourself; what could go right? Change the story that you are seeing into something that helps you. Doing this can get your mind off of the fear and whatever it is that is creating the fear, and will switch your mind to something else. Remember, your brain is like a computer, searching for anything and everything it can to bring you the information you are searching for. When you dwell on fear, worry, lack, you will see more evidence of it and create more stories around it. But when you change the story of fear and what it means about you as a human being, you will begin to notice that fear doesn't keep you stuck anymore. Remember, fear is neither bad nor good. It just is. When fear comes up and bubbles out of your subconscious mind this gives you a chance to reframe and change the story about the fear you're feeling.

Follow the Fear

This is the one trick your ego will never see coming because it goes against what most people are willing to do. Follow the fear. By following the fear, you are following the story that was created around a certain situation, and by following the story you are able to unwrap it and see it for what it truly is. Which then allows you to decide if it's helpful to you or not.

Here's an example; let's say you have a fear of speaking in front of a group of more than 10 people. The story goes something like this:

"I'm afraid that I'll stumble over my words or people will think I'm stupid or my voice sounds weird or I might blush and then everyone will make fun of me."

Follow the fear by asking yourself some questions.

"What makes me think people will make fun of me?"

"Well, when I was in 5th grade I stood in front of the class and..."

Continue following the story and begin dismantling it.

"Okay. I am no longer in 5th grade, I have more tools and confidence now than I did back then. I have better friends and

I can choose to turn these nerves into excitement. I also have no control over other people but I do have total control over myself. So, what can I do to make this more fun?"

By asking yourself questions and following the road the fear has created you will be able to see just how silly the fear actually is and you'll even begin to see a solution to dismantle and clear up the fear. I like doing this because you can do it with yourself or even have a trusted friend ask you these questions and really help you talk out the fear.

Overthinkers Anonymous: Fear's Slightly Less Obnoxious Twin

If your Google search history looks something like; what to do when you say the wrong thing to someone, why aren't they texting me back, how to stop embarrassing yourself in front of strangers - you might be an overthinker. By now, you've probably realized that your pesky ego is behind all this overthinking stuff and you're right, it is. I'm not saying that overthinking is inherently bad or good. But if it's controlling your life like it did mine in the past, chances are it's time to give unnecessary overthinking the boot.

I used to identify as an overthinker. I said I was a worrier. That's just who I was. Notice the identity language there keeping me stuck. My mom was an overthinker, her mom was, so naturally, I grabbed hold of this identity like a ratty hand-me-down pair of jeans. And I didn't think twice about it. Until it left me so afraid to leave my own house, it was literally taking over my life.

I realized right then and there that I had two choices. I could wait for a knight in shining armor to come rescue me (i.e. something or someone external to change my circumstances), or I could suit up and slay the dragon myself. I am giving you this choice because let me promise you, if you choose to wait for someone else to do this for you, you'll be waiting longer than any princess in a castle.

If you've chosen the latter, which is way more fun by the way, here are a few ways to slay your overthinking dragon.

- **Become Aware of your Triggers**

  There are going to be certain people, places, or things that set off your radar and begin the inevitable tailspin of thoughts that clog up your brain. The key is to become aware of them. Once you recognize what it is that triggers overthinking, you can stop the thoughts before they get out of hand.

- **Minimize Decisions**

  We make thousands of decisions a day. And that's just consciously. The more decisions we have to make, the harder it is for us to make them. Eliminate small decisions by giving yourself 5 seconds or less to decide. Seriously, 5 seconds or less. Should I go do the dishes? What should I wear today? Should I go and talk to my boss about a raise? 5 SECONDS OR LESS.

- **Disrupt your Thoughts**

  Your thoughts will run wild if you allow them to so as soon as you become aware of them throw in a wrench to clog the gears. Stop, listen now, that's right, your thoughts are clearing now. These are all ways to speak to your subconscious mind and give your conscious mind – the part that is doing the overthinking – a break, and by disrupting the pattern of thinking, the thoughts will ease.

- **Ask the Right Questions**

  Oftentimes when overthinking thoughts pile in, they are very generalized. You can nip these generalized thoughts in the bud by asking yourself questions. Always? Never? Is that really true? What would happen if it did work out? What would happen if it didn't? Asking questions is another way to move your conscious mind out of the way and allow your subconscious to speak up and give you an answer.

Journal Prompts:

Use these journal prompts to help yourself overcome fear when it shows up in your life. Remember, asking yourself questions helps you to see the solution that may be buried under the surface of the problem.

1. What situation or circumstance is bringing up this fear?

    a) What about this situation is causing me to feel fear? Chances are, it's not the situation itself, but what it means if you don't get the outcome you want.

    b) Is this story my own or someone else's?

2. Can I change the meaning of this fear into an emotion that will be more beneficial to me? Such as reframing nervousness into excitement.

3. Have I tried following the fear story to expose it, reframe it, and evaluate it to see if it's something I need or not?

4. When this fear comes up do I notice self-sabotaging patterns around it? This requires a lot of self-awareness.

5. Are there a lot of similar situations in which I notice fear coming up for me?

F.E.A.R

False evidence appearing real. Change the story you are telling yourself about fear and how you see fear will change.

CHAPTER 11

TAPPING INTO THE UNIVERSE

I can already feel it, even just the name of this chapter makes you uncomfortable. I mean the Universe? What is all this? You may even be thinking that you're not religious so you don't want to discuss this at all. Maybe you even slammed this book shut and vowed never to touch it again or threw it across the room like a piece of hot coal. But if you're still here, hear me out because this, combined with the ego mind stuff in the previous chapters, is what began to change my entire life. And it happened really quickly.

It's no secret that there are a million and one opinions about why we are here, if we are alone in this world, and how we were created. For the people who believe in "this stuff" there are many different names we give to what, or who, we believe in. God, Spirit, Universe, Angels, Source. Regardless of what you call it, the fact remains that we believe we are not alone and we were put here for a reason that is much larger than we can even comprehend.

I get it. I didn't used to believe in all this "woo, woo" stuff and I just went on my merry way living life like everyone was out to get me, crying about my broke ass every single night, spending time with people who would be considered the villain in any horror movie, and living my life in a daze of confusion, pain, and quiet sorrow. It wasn't until I applied both the mindset work from the previous chapters, and tapping into the Universe, that I began to notice massive changes. Like really freaking big ones. Getting a book deal, working with dream clients that seemed to appear out of nowhere, my business taking off, my financial situation sorting itself out, winning contests left and right, and my ego sitting in the corner more quietly than she ever had before... just to name a few. Not to mention actually loving my life instead of just faking a smile until I could retreat back into the comfy place inside my head once more.

Believing, even just for a second, that there is something much larger out there helping you succeed takes the giant pressure of life off your shoulders and helps to disperse the weight a little bit. Seriously, if you feel like you're carrying the world on your shoulders right now, at least allow the belief that there is something bigger out there helping you creep in just for a second or even just for the purposes of this chapter. You might also be wondering why tapping into the Universe is so important because you've done fine so far without it, thank you very much. Remember that chapter on the subconscious mind and how incredibly powerful your thoughts and subconscious programming are? Well, your subconscious mind is actually in cahoots with the Universe. It's kind of like your subconscious mind has a huge mega phone held up against the Universe's ear and whatever is programmed subconsciously is told to the Universe and thus shows up in your physical reality as a physical manifestation.

Here's the tricky, sticky thing; whether you believe in the Universe or a higher power at all, it, along with its Universal Laws, are always working. This can be a scary thought and you may want to immediately run to the sink and try to wash out your brain with a bar of soap. The realization that your thoughts have this much power can be intimidating but on the other side of that is the idea that whatever you can think about you can bring into your life. That is the mighty power of the Universe.

The Universe and the world of quantum physics are a complicated topic and you might think that in order to fully tap into this magical world of the Universe and Universal Intelligence you have to know anything and everything about it in order for it to work. That's just your ego showing up by the way. Think about how many things in life you use without fully understanding how they work. Every day you flick on the electricity without a second thought as to how those little waves of electric energy are flowing through your walls. You don't go jumping out of planes without a parachute because you know gravity isn't going to allow you to float in midair, but you don't really know the inner workings of gravity. You just trust it to work. You tap away on your phone without understanding the innermost mechanics of it. And yet, all these things work without our full conscious thinking.

While you may not want to study electricity or gravity or even your iPhone, understanding how the Universe uses your thoughts to manifest your physical reality can be a very helpful thing to do. In fact, it gives you a lot of power, which is really exciting to say the least. Once you understand how your thoughts can literally create anything and everything you see, you will be more likely to watch what you think and say in private. Which the ego takes a personal offense to by the way.

Everything was once created by a thought. This book you are reading came directly from the Universe into my head which then led me to writing it down on paper, taking it to a publisher and getting it printed for your enjoyment. My book was a literal manifestation from the Universe. But let's take a step further back into the past. The very first patented telephone was invented by Alexander Graham Bell in 1876. This was a very unusual invention at the time and we can only imagine the scandal surrounding such an idea. I mean seriously, someone had the audacity to think of an invention that allowed people to give someone else a message over this thing called a phone instead of running up a giant hill both ways. Which was unheard of at the time. But he made it anyway, because he had an idea that he couldn't let go of. And he knew just how much it would help people.

The Wright brothers had an idea for an invention that could fly people through the air and make long distance travel less time consuming (I'm just paraphrasing, I'm sure they had a much more eloquent way of saying this back then). The first homes were built because someone thought about a place that had a roof and four walls. Cars were made from the thought that walking everywhere sucks (again, just paraphrasing here).

All of these inventions that we use on a daily basis were created by the Universe and then put into someone's mind. A thought was born out of a feeling which then led to a belief that life could be better with a particular invention and thus, physical action was taken to bring this new invention to life. If you have a thought about something, it's already being created on a quantum level and it is brought to your physical reality via your vibration and physical action. Everything in this Universe is made up of vibrating atoms and they are vibrating at such a fast pace that things appear to be solid. This computer I'm typing on, the headphones I'm wearing, the chair I'm sitting in, your dog taking a snooze in the sunshine, your car in the garage, the money in your pockets, all of it is vibrating. Including you. Life is like a flip book made up of small things that when moved quickly enough, look like one solid moving piece.

The Universe has twelve immutable laws, and probably many more, but there are three laws that stand out the most. The Law of Attraction, the Law of Vibration and the Law of Action. One of the most polarizing laws of the Universe is the Law of Attraction. Love it or hate it, the Law of Attraction is always working; it's up to your thoughts, feelings, beliefs, and vibration to determine if it works in your favor or not. The Law of Attraction simply states that like attracts like. Meaning like thoughts attract like thoughts, feelings attract similar feelings, and so on. Pretty simple law.

The Law of Vibration states that everything in this universe is vibrating. Including your thoughts, feelings, and beliefs, and the frequency of those vibrations is based on how they make you feel. And how something makes you feel is based on your subconscious programming around that particular thing. Everything you want is also vibrating at a certain frequency. Think of a radio. If you want to tune into 106.3, your radio station has to be on the right frequency. Which means if your thoughts, feelings and beliefs do not match the frequency of what you desire, it will be challenging to call them into your life.

One of the laws that most people seem to forget about, or don't know exists, is The Law of Action. Which states that no physical manifestation can happen without physical action. Sorry to crush your dreams of sitting on your couch all day dreaming about a Ferrari and having it magically poof into your living room. As you know, the action part is usually where your ego pops in and stops you in your tracks with massive self-sabotage, but knowing what you know now, you are much better equipped at dismantling your ego mind and using this law to your advantage.

All of these Universal Laws come back to your thoughts and feelings and the meaning you give them. The Universe is literally using your thoughts and feelings as the blueprint of your life and then rearranging the pieces to fit the vision rolling around inside your head. There is nothing more powerful than the thoughts you think and the feelings you feel, and the more in-tune you become with your thoughts and feelings, the more fun working with the Universe becomes. And the better your life begins to look.

The Law of Attraction Explained

I want to take a bit of a deeper dive into the Law of Attraction simply because it's one of the most popular laws of the Universe, and due to its simplistic nature it draws in a lot of cynics and critics. Not only that but there is a lot of misinformation floating around out there about this law too. I mean, when I first learned about this law I truly believed if I sat on my couch and thought really hard about the car I wanted it would just poof into my living room all on its own.

The fact of the matter is, there are more laws at work when manifesting, or using the Law of Attraction, to call in whatever it is you desire. Which, by the way, can be literally anything. If it's in your head and heart, you can manifest it. But for simplicity's sake, let's stick with the Law of Attraction and break it down just a bit. As I said, the Law of Attraction states that "like attracts like". Similar to a magnet. If you're angry, you will notice and attract more things that make you angry. If you're happy, you'll take notice and attract more things that make you happy. This isn't to say that if you have one negative thought about someone cutting you off your whole day is screwed. The point is to take notice of the thoughts you have throughout the day, decide if they're hurting you or helping you, learn from them, and release them if needed. All thoughts and feelings have a purpose and a message for you. The point isn't to ignore them.

Now back to the Law of Attraction. Like attracts like. That is the simplest way to describe the Law of Attraction. When you first begin recognizing this idea, you begin to take notice of your manifestations. A manifestation is simply a thought brought into fruition in your physical reality. Manifestation happens on a daily and continuous basis whether you're aware of it or not. But there is a way to consciously use the Law of Attraction. And it really only requires three steps.

- Ask
- Believe
- Receive

Ask for what you want, believe it's possible, have faith it's coming, trust, release it, and then do everything you can to become a match for what you desire on a mental and physical level. I told you it was simple! Of course, it gets a little muddy there in the middle with the whole believing thing and then becoming a match for what you want, but it's not as complicated as it may seem on the surface.

Think of it like this, you go to a restaurant, scan the menu for whatever sounds the best and order your meal. You trust that the waiter will bring you what you ordered. You're not concerned about what the cook is doing, how long it's going to take, or if your meal will come at all. You also don't run into the back every five minutes anxiously asking when your food is coming. Doing so would annoy the staff and you'd probably be asked to leave which means you'd have to go to another restaurant and start all over again. Which just adds even more time to getting what you desired.

Once you order, or ask in this case, for what you want, trust it's coming to you no matter what. While it's being prepared for you, get ready for its arrival. If it's food you asked for, your body gets ready to eat this food by creating more saliva in the mouth and preparing the stomach. If you desire to manifest a new car, get prepared for that new car. Start looking for the car you want. Go to a dealership and test drive a few. Make a space in your driveway. Prepare yourself on a mental level for this car by releasing resistance around having it. The more you can focus on yourself and being the best *you* you can be, the faster the Law of Attraction will work in your favor.

The Truth about Manifestation

Manifestation is kind of a buzz word lately. You hear it in Facebook groups, from the gurus, from Podcasts, and basically anything to do with spirituality and personal development. You also hear people saying things like, "I think I manifested that." Or, "I didn't even manifest it but there it was." The thing is, you're always manifesting. No matter how hard you are "trying" or "not trying". Manifestation means bringing something into your physical reality that was first created in your mind. That's it.

Consciously or subconsciously and based on your vibration and frequency. So yeah, everything is a manifestation. Everything. That's just how this Universe works.

Now the question becomes, can you be more intentional with your manifestations? Yes, of course! Let's say you want to manifest an extra $50 for some holiday gifts for your family. You don't need any fancy spells, crystals, pendulums, candles, or a wand for this to work. Simply set an intention by saying something along the lines of, "I intend to manifest $50 for holiday gifts." Then go about your day. That's it. There's no need to overcomplicate things. You don't have to go around yelling affirmations at yourself all day for this to work either.

The part that trips a lot of people up, including myself when I first learned about all this, is wondering how long it will take. How long will it take for me to get this manifestation?? I was very impatient. Which only prolongs the waiting time by the way. Remember the Law of Vibration? Well the faster you can trust that the money (or whatever you're manifesting) is on the way, the more quickly your vibration will match whatever it is you're manifesting which helps to bring it into your life that much more quickly. Think about it. When you think of a song you'd like to hear on the radio, within a few minutes you're rocking out, head swinging, hands in the air to your favorite song. It's because you had no attachment to it. You didn't create a meaning about it happening or not happening. You just thought hey, that'd be cool to hear.

Now think about a time when you really wanted that special person to text you. You waited by your phone all day and all night. Checking it every few seconds. You could feel your heart pumping faster and faster with every tick of the clock. Then without fail, the fear rises in your chest and screams lies in your ears of all the meanings behind the text not popping up on your screen. Maybe the text comes in a week later, maybe it doesn't at all. The point is, the more attached you are to an outcome and the bigger the meaning you give to your manifestation, the longer it's going to take to manifest into your life. Set the intention, trust that it's coming and go on about your life.

How to Get Tapped into your Thoughts and the Universe

1. Get Quiet and Observe your Thoughts at Least Once a Day

Meditation is one of the easiest ways to become aware of the thoughts you have running amuck inside your head. The biggest mistake most people make when meditating is trying to control the thoughts popping up. What you resist persists. Allow them to be there, let them float on by and then recenter yourself by focusing on your breath. Use an app like Headspace or the Calm app to practice meditation and simply sit quietly for 10 minutes every single day.

2. Recognize You are Not your Thoughts

We have billions of thoughts run through our mind on a daily basis and while we aren't consciously aware of most of them (that would be awful), the ones we do recognize we tend to take personally. Or should I say, your ego takes them personally. If you are thinking angry thoughts, or having a thought run around and around in your head like a hamster on a wheel, take three deep breaths, say out loud or in your head, "I am not my thoughts, I am having a thought about [blank] but that is not who I am." By doing this, you are giving voice to your ego and your thoughts while recognizing that you are simply HAVING a thought, but that thought is not who you are. Go back to chapter 10 if you're having fear based thoughts.

3. Trust your Intuition

Your intuitive thoughts, feelings, and nudges are messages from the Universe pushing you to move forward or take an action that could move you in a very positive direction. Listen to those nudges and trust that they are taking you on the right path.

4. Trust and Have Faith

Jump and the net will appear. Faith happens when it looks like it's not working. This is the most challenging for your ego but it is the one thing that will get you tapped into the Universe more quickly than anything else. Trust that whatever is unfolding in your life, wanted or unwanted, is happening for your highest good and is happening to either teach you a lesson or move you forward in a way that will bring you an abundance of blessings. If you can put your trust into your phone for working, or your car for driving you where you need to go, you can put your trust into yourself and the Universe to bring you the life you desire.

5. Check in with Your Feelings

Feelings. You either love them or hate them but they are one of the best tells of if you are on the right track or not. When you are tapped into the Universe, you feel good. Great even. You are feeling all the positive things you want to be feeling. When you're plugged into your ego, you feel worry, lack, and fear. This is not to say that when you are tapped into the Universe it will be butterflies and rainbows all day everyday; but you won't feel the frantic worry, lack and fear that the ego creates. Take note of your feelings on a daily basis and do what you can to change the way you feel such as moving, exercise, mediation, thinking of something that makes you happy, anything that changes your mood into a positive one.

"The Universe does not:

Trick us.

Deceive us.

Play games.

We either get exactly what we asked for or exactly what we need to move to a new level."

CHAPTER 12

YOUR DREAM LIFE IS
GOING TO COST YOU

Your ego will have you believe that you can have your cake and eat it too. And you can, just not in the way your ego thinks. You see, your ego believes that you can stay in your comfy comfort zone, that you don't have to change anything or be open or even do anything differently to get what you want. Here's a tip, you CAN have your cake and eat it too but you're going to have to be willing to make some changes around here, which come in the form of letting go. The idea that you might have to let go of those beliefs you've been holding onto so tightly they've left bruises on your hands is about as terrifying to your ego as jumping into a pit of spiders. Why would you want to do that when life is all non-spidery over here? Here's the thing; you can't hold onto your old life if you're going to create a new one. You're going to have to let it go. And when I say your old life I'm really talking about the beliefs, values, and identities that created that life.

Remember that whole chapter on the subconscious mind? Well that is where your beliefs, values, and identities are stored and they are created from stories that we heard and saw as children. Our ego latched onto these stories like a calf drinking its mother's milk, and took them in as the whole truth, and nothing but the truth. But the ego took it one step further and decided that every story we ever watched play out or heard as children was personal, and she created a meaning about those stories and what they meant about who you are. If your dad wasn't around you may have made that mean you weren't lovable. Or worthy of being loved. If kids made fun of you for being shy and quiet all the time that meant you were the outcast, the kid no one wanted to play with on the playground.

You hold onto these identities throughout your childhood and sometimes even into adulthood. They stick with you like molasses in the summer time until you consciously choose to release them. The thing is, these beliefs, values, and identities are buried in the subconscious mind so it's hard to see them. If you look really closely though, they're there. Just as they always have been. They make their way to the surface and show their faces in your relationships, the way you think, your internal dialogue, your actions and eventually as your entire external reality.

You may be wondering why you wouldn't banish these old beliefs, values, and identities if you simply didn't need them anymore, but if it were that simple wouldn't everyone be doing it? These beliefs, values, and identities show up as truth in your life. And to your ego, being right is everything. They show up as the stories you live by and until you recognize they are nothing but a story you will continue to create a life based on them.

Maybe it's because I'm a writer, or maybe it's just because I love analogies and metaphors, but your life is literally a book filled with stories. Stories that someone made up, plopped into your head and once you were old enough, you continued to write them. You might be consciously thinking, yeah right and rolling your eyes at me but think about it. Stories play out all day long. They roll from your tongue when you're not thinking, they plaster themselves to the walls of your brain as thoughts, they play out like a little puppet show in front of your very eyes. The reason you don't notice them is because they are wrapped in a golden truth bow. So, you don't question them. And because your subconscious mind is the best working computer on the market, it does everything in its power to ensure you are right by finding evidence of whatever it is you believe and whatever it is that aligns with your identity.

"Life is hard, money is tough to come by, we're just not those types of people, nothing ever works out for us/me, I just wasn't lucky enough for that." These are the stories of your past that your ego is clinging onto for dear life because without them who would you be? If your ego can't figure out who you are and slap a little label on you, it feels like it can't breathe, like it can't survive. So, your ego uses stories to decide who you are, what beliefs you should have, how you should show up in your life and ultimately, what your life should look like. If you want to throw a big F you to your ego, change the stories you are telling to yourself. Like most things, this is easier said than done and your ego will throw a temper tantrum louder than anything you've ever heard but if you want to live that big bold life, you're going to have to learn to let go of things that no longer serve you. Growth is uncomfortable but so is living a life that you don't love.

One of the most frustrating things is to look in the mirror and realize you're the one that's sabotaging your life. On a conscious level you want more money, a bigger house, a super-hot significant other that adores you, or hell, even just to be happy and fulfilled, but on the inside, your subconscious mind is brewing up a stew of self-sabotage and frog legs that your ego will serve up to you on a silver platter of truth. It's so much easier to turn the mirror on others and say,

"You're doing this to me!"

And continue to blame other people for every little problem in your life. Which I've done by the way. I've got news for you, if you've been waiting not so patiently for that shiny knight on a white stallion to come and save you, you'll be waiting forever. The only person who can change your life is you. And the only person sabotaging the life of your dreams is you. I realize that is basically a giant horse pill and if you're anything like me, trying to swallow pills is like trying to swallow an everlasting gum ball from Willy Wonka's Chocolate Factory. It isn't easy, but it's something you have to do. The point is, this chapter is about turning the mirror on yourself, seeing your beliefs, values and identities for what they truly are and molding them like clay to fit the life you've always wanted.

How to Identify Limiting Beliefs and Stories

Your stories and beliefs don't come out just at night like a lurking vampire, they're there, standing right in front of you, looking you dead in the eye. You're just so used to them that you don't even notice what they look or sound like anymore. Identifying them requires you to question your thoughts, words, and actions in any area of your life that you are less than thrilled about.

Think about any area of your life that you aren't happy about. What beliefs do you notice you have around that area? Do you hear yourself saying certain things that do not align with the outcome you want?

Example:

Consciously: You want more money

Subconsciously: You hold lack beliefs around money that were programmed into your subconscious mind by watching and listening to the people around you.

How you speak about money:

- Money is hard to come by
- Only certain people have money
- Money sucks
- I hate money

How you feel around money:

- Uncomfortable
- Sad, angry or frustrated, unless it comes around a lot
- Afraid or scared
- Lack like there's not enough to go around

Physical manifestation:

- Struggle keeping money
- Struggle Attracting money
- Have a hard time saving money

Every single belief shows up in our actions and our actions are something that we can physically see. Take note of your actions as well in areas of your life that you're not happy with.

Work Backwards:

If your life is a result of your actions and your actions are a result of your beliefs, values, and identity, take a look at the actions you are taking when it comes to a certain area of your life.

What actions or behaviors are you taking that are resulting in the outcome you are getting?

What thoughts create those actions?

What beliefs align with those thoughts?

What identity have you created around those thoughts, beliefs and actions? Identity shows up as "I am" statements.

What values do you hold around those areas of your life that you wished were different? Do those values align with the outcome you want?

Check in on your Internal Thoughts, Words, & Pictures:

Your reality is created by your own internal representation of everything that happens in your life. This means that everyone's reality is a bit different simply because everyone has had different external situations and put different meanings on those things. Great, so knowing that, it means you can change your reality by changing your internal representation of reality.

Remember, if you want something different, create it in your mind first. This means taking stock of the thoughts, words, and images rolling around in your head. When something happens outside of you, do you automatically go to a negative or self-limiting place? This is for you to become aware of so that you can change it.

Take Note of Reasons

Reasons why you can't do something are limiting beliefs wearing a mask. If you've ever found yourself saying, "Yeah but...", "I don't have enough..." or, "I can't do that because..." These are all limiting beliefs disguised as excuses.

You might even be throwing some reasons down at me right now as you're reading this. Hey, I didn't say pulling out your limiting beliefs and serving them raw on a platter was going to be easy. I just said it's necessary to let go of them in order to live the big, bold life that you've always wanted. You have all the resources you need to have everything you want; you just have to put your focus on them.

Once you've peeled back the layers of the onion to show its meaty middle, it's time to release the beliefs that no longer serve you. This sounds like it'd take years to do and to be honest, some of the deeper seeded beliefs may take longer, but for the purposes of this book, here is a simple, belief-busting script that I learned from Michael Stevenson, my NLP Practitioner instructor, that you can use to at least untangle the spider web of beliefs hold up in your mind:

1. What is the belief that you would like to change?

Before you can change a belief, you must first know what it is you want to change. Finding this belief can be as easy as looking at what you want and asking yourself why you don't yet have it. The answers that come up will be some of the beliefs you have around what it means to get whatever it is you want. Focus on changing one belief at a time and start with the one that came up first, as that is the one that most likely holds the most weight. And removing it will help to dismantle the rest of them. Like dominos.

2. **Why do you believe that?** Asking this question can help you realize where the belief came from because chances are, it's not even your own belief.

3. **What are you afraid would happen if you didn't believe that?** If you stopped believing the original belief, what would happen?

4. **Do you believe that?** As in, do you believe that fear from question three to be true?

5. **Is that your belief?** Again, asking this question makes us think about if these beliefs are even ours, and beliefs that are not our own can be easier to release.

6. **What is the new belief that I choose to believe instead that empowers me?** Replace the old belief with something new that makes you feel good, supports your goals, and aligns with the life you want to live.

There are a million and one belief busting scripts that you can use to overcome beliefs and as I said, this may not completely pull out the belief but it will at least disrupt it and make you begin to question it. The point is to keep asking yourself questions until the belief you had no longer makes sense to keep around, then replace it with a new, empowering belief that serves you better.

You always want to make sure to add in a new empowering belief after removing an old one. Think about it like pulling out a really big sliver. Once the sliver is out now there's a hole where it used to be. If your body didn't fill and heal that hole with skin and tissue, more dirt and debris could fill it up again. And nobody wants that.

It is 100% possible to change the stories you are telling yourself to fit the mold you want. We hold onto these stories because we believe we need them in order to stay inside the box we've created for ourselves. When in reality, we don't need a box at all. Be willing to rewrite your stories and you will see your life change.

Become Really Good at Flipping the Script

Chances are, you're not going to walk around with that belief busting script in your back pocket and every time you feel a negative belief popping back up you squat down in the middle of the street and work through it in your journal. I'm not one for absolutes and I'm also not one to say there is only one way to do things, so here are some other ways to huff and puff and blow down the walls of your limiting beliefs.

Questions:

I've said it before and I'll say it again, ask questions all the time! Seriously. Get really good at asking yourself questions. As soon as you notice a reason popping up, flip it and ask yourself what you can do to find the resources needed.

Change your Focus:

Whatever you give your attention to is what is going to continue popping up. When you focus on everything going wrong, that's all you see. Think of a time in a movie when the main character, after having a tough day says something along the lines of, "What else could go wrong??" While looking longing up at the sky. And they get caught in the rain, a car drives by and splashes mud on them... you know the story.

Where you put your focus is very important because simply put, you get what you focus on most. So why wouldn't you choose to focus on what you want and desire out of life?

EFT:

EFT stands for Emotional Freedom Technique and it is used as a form of releasing pent up negative energy in the body. This type of therapy is loosely based on acupuncture and instead of needles, EFT uses your own hands and pressure to tap on certain points of your body. Tapping on these areas of your body helps to release the stuck or stagnant energy and allows the energy to move freely throughout the body. EFT can be used to simply get you out of a stuck state or feeling. Such as lack of motivation, anger, sadness, frustration, nervousness and any other emotion that you'd like. You can also use it to release limiting beliefs and the emotions associated with them. I have even personally used the EFT Tapping to release the pain associated with migraines I was having. And it worked really quickly. I've also used it to relieve stress and anxious emotions when I was in a pinch and needed something quick.

EFT is extremely simple to do on yourself and it only takes three minutes to complete. There are 8 points you tap on during the technique and 1 point you tap on as the set up. The first area you begin tapping on is called the Karate Chop Point which is located on the side of your hand. Next is on the inner part of your eye brow on your brown bone. Then the side of your eye, under your eye, under your nose on your cupid's bow, under your bottom lip, under your collar bone, under your arm, near the "bra strap" area on your side near your back and finally, on the crown of your head. Going through all these points consecutively is considered one round.

While you are tapping on each point make sure you are applying pressure with two fingers. You of course don't want to hurt yourself but find a happy medium of pressure so that the energy is able to move throughout your body and you are able to feel the relief. You also want to make sure you are focusing on the problem you want to alleviate while tapping. Your thoughts are very powerful and this is what helps move the emotion. I'll give you an example tapping session/script:

Step One:

Gauge your problem/emotion on a scale of 1-10. 10 being the worst pain, problem, or emotion you have ever experienced in your life, and 1 being totally over it. The goal is to get below a 4 with one round. If that doesn't happen, you can go through a few more rounds as needed.

Step Two:

The Setup is used before beginning the sequence and is done only once. **Do this before every single session.** While holding one of your hands upright, begin tapping with the opposite hand on the Karate Chop point or the side of your hand. While tapping on this point repeat this phrase three times through, "Even though I have this (problem, emotion, etc.), I deeply and completely accept myself."

Step Three:

Begin the EFT sequence which involves tapping on the 8 points of your body I stated above. Begin with the eyebrow, then the side of your eye, under your eye, under your nose, under your bottom lip, under your collar bone, under your arm near the "bra strap" area and finally, around the crown of your head. While tapping keep your focus on the problem and repeat it out loud. For example, "This anger, this anger, this anger, this anger." Tap on each point for a few seconds before moving onto the next. Once you finish one round, you can do a second one before moving on. I personally find two rounds is more than enough.

Step Four:

Very similar to the last step but instead of focusing on the problem and repeating the problem out loud while tapping, you repeat your favorite affirmation or positive suggestion. Such as, "I am in full control of my feelings and emotions and I choose to feel good today." Again, do this while tapping on all 8 points of your body. You only need to do this for one round.

Once you have completed all the rounds then evaluate your problem again on a scale of 1-10 and if it is not below a 4, go through the entire sequence again.

Hypnosis:

Hypnosis is another way to release negative emotions and limiting beliefs quickly and effectively if you're short on time. Hypnosis is similar to meditation but pushes your conscious mind out of the way. It's kind of like a vacation for your conscious mind, allowing your subconscious mind to open up and fully listen to positive suggestions without the chatter of the ego. Hypnosis is so effective because it bypasses the critical factor (your filter) and allows yourself or a hypnotherapist to install new empowering beliefs quickly and easily. And yes, you can in fact practice hypnosis on yourself just as easily as you can practice meditation or a breathing exercise.

There is a lot to hypnosis, seriously a lot. I spent over 10 hours of training on it to fully understand everything there is to know about it. Of course, there are a million and one misconceptions around hypnosis because it's just not talked about as much as meditation is. I won't be diving into each and every fear or worry surrounding hypnosis but I will say this; you will be in control 100% of the time, yes, you will probably be able to hear everything the hypnotherapist is saying, no you are not asleep, no you will not do anything you don't want to do. The thing is, most of us are already in a state of hypnosis and we don't even realize it. When you're sitting at your desk while your eyes glaze over from looking at the computer for more than five hours, and your mind begins to drift, you are slowly getting into a state of hypnosis. TV also puts you into a hypnotic state.

You can do hypnosis on yourself or watch guided hypnosis videos but I do highly recommend going to a hypnotherapist that knows what they are doing so that all you have to do is sit there and relax while your limiting beliefs and bad habits melt away. But if you really want to learn to do it yourself, or are just curious to take a deep dive into the history of hypnosis and what it all entails, you can read Learn Hypnosis Now! By Michael Stevenson, which is a fantastic book that gives you the literal ins and outs of hypnosis.

There is no shortage of ways to release limiting beliefs. Some of them require another person such as a qualified coach, and others just require yourself, some time, and a whole lot of awareness. Releasing limiting beliefs and thoughts is an ongoing process.

While you can get rid of limiting beliefs and limiting behaviors quickly and easily with the techniques I've listed out above, as you progress in life and move into a new level, new beliefs and behaviors will come up to the surface. The goal is to ensure you have the tools to release and be aware of any limiting beliefs and behaviors that are holding you back in any area of your life and for all levels of your life. Remember to be conscious of what you say, what you think, and how you act, and you will begin to uncover the beliefs that may be holding you back.

One last thing to remember when releasing limiting beliefs - These beliefs have served you for a long time. Years sometimes. It can feel scary to "get rid of" some of them and you may even feel like you need to keep them for protection. Because to your ego, they *were* protecting you. And while that may be true, they were also protecting you from living a really incredible life and you don't need them to protect you anymore.

If you're noticing resistance when releasing these old beliefs, or your ego is trying to drop in and convince you that you need these beliefs to keep you physically safe, remember this; your flight or fight response never fails. You literally have a built-in mechanism that keeps you alive. Your ego is just telling you another story to keep you in your comfort zone. Ignore her words and realize it's okay to let old beliefs go that no longer serve you. You don't need them anymore.

"You will only get as far as you believe you can."

CHAPTER 13

LET YOUR HIGHER SELF BE YOUR GUIDE

Have you ever had a feeling that you should do something in particular? Like a nagging pull that wouldn't leave you alone until you did it? Calling into the emergency room because your Grandma was acting "strange" and slurring her words, which ended up inevitably saving her life. Checking on your basement window (which you literally never do) only to find a trapped baby bunny that you were able to save and pull out of harm's way. Walking down a street you don't normally go down only to find a magical little hole in the wall you didn't even know existed.

You think to yourself, "How lucky am I?" or, "What a coincidence!"

This pull, nudge, or feeling is your intuition guiding you to do the things that will bring you closer to the person you were meant to be. Uh...Whaaaa?? This can sound a little "woo woo" if you will so let me throw some science on this first. In quantum physics, every scenario already exists. Meaning, the version of you who has well, whatever it is you want out of life, already exists. Even more than that, any and every possibility or scenario has already happened and whatever one you see is based on your focus, beliefs, thoughts, feelings, and actions. Your higher self, your intuition, uses nudges, feelings, and thoughts to help you tap into that version of yourself - the best possible version of you. The problem is that these nudges are usually drowned out by the screaming voice of your pessimistic ego mind. Which is why I had you do so much work and understand your ego before you get to this point because if I didn't, your ego would toss this out with the trash too.

How many times a day do you have a random thought pop into your head about a brilliant idea, or see a house for sale that just might be your dream home, or think about a friend you haven't heard from in ages and think about acting on all these things but instead of doing that, you choose to listen to the voice that says, you can't afford it, your friend is fine, your idea isn't so brilliant after all? Imagine for a second if you had acted on those nudges. Where would you be? What would you be doing?

Your higher self or the version of you that has everything you desire in life is pushing you to take action, pushing you to do the things you've been meant to do all along. It's like a game of Candy Land. You move your piece around the board unit you get to Candy Land Castle at the end. Sometimes you get to move five places forward, other times you move three steps back. And sometimes you get stuck in some mud. Either way, you're always moving, growing, and learning. The only time you're ever truly moving backwards is when you stop listening to your intuition completely and start using your ego as your trail map. Even then, there's a lesson to be learned. I'm mixing my analogies here but you get the point.

If you're anything like me, you spent your whole life looking out a window that had a filter over it that only allowed you to see the pain, the bad in the world, the struggle, the rain clouds and maybe on a few special occasions, the sun. Tapping into your higher self is like looking out a window and seeing the world in a completely different way for the first time ever. And when you see things differently, the things you see change. When you allow your higher self to be the filter for all of the decisions you make, all the thoughts you think, and the feelings you feel, you show up from that point of view, as if everything was already rigged in your favor because everything you want has already happened successfully.

Showing up as your higher self has less to do with what you are doing but so much more to do with who you are *being*. Using the same window analogy, think about two people looking out the same window and seeing a deer on their front lawn. One person is operating from their ego and the other is operating from their higher self. The person who is focused on the problem (ego mind), sees the deer and gets angry about it trespassing on their property. The person who is focused on living from their highest self, sees the deer and is in awe of the beauty of nature. This may be a silly example but which person do you think is living the life they want? Take it one step further - two people are standing at the bottom of a trail with the same equipment. One person says it's simply not possible to walk the trail because they don't have the right equipment. The other person tries anyway with what they have, learning what they need for the next time they come to walk this trail.

Another way to think about embodying your higher self is to think about your mind as an old school movie projector.

Whatever thoughts you have rummaging around in there and the meanings you have about those thoughts will be projected out into your life, like that of a movie on a screen. If you want to change the movie you are watching, i.e., your life, you have to embody the version of yourself who has the life you want. Meaning embodying their thoughts, feelings, beliefs, habits, behaviors, words, and actions. A prime example of this is professional athletes. They use visualization as part of their training techniques. They see themselves winning the race. The feel of the wind on their face. The noise of the crowd cheering, yelling their name. The way their muscles ache from pushing through to the finish line. They can even feel the sweat on their face and see people running up to them ready to embrace.

They make it feel so real that the subconscious mind has no choice but to make it actually happen. If you win 100 times in your mind first, it will be a lot easier to win in real life. If you remember from the chapter on the subconscious mind, your subconscious does not know the difference between real (physical) and imagined (in your mind). If you want a particular outcome - winning the race, losing weight, making x amount of dollars - see it, feel it, believe it in your mind first. And by doing so you are literally changing the movie that is being projected.

At this point, your higher self may sound like a mythical unicorn standing at the end of a rainbow with a pot of gold in its mouth. But she's not as far fetched as she sounds because she is you in your truest form. Meaning she's you without the old programming that no longer serves you. Without the stories of your past holding you back. Your higher self is the version of you who takes risks because she knows everything is rigged in her favor. She doesn't let fear or judgement get in her way. She gets into alignment before making decisions to ensure she is not making a decision out of lack, scarcity, or fear. But she also doesn't sit on action, and makes decisions quickly. She sees problems as a way to learn and grow and as a stepping stone to the next level. She believes in herself and sees her true potential. Just as your ego is a filter in which you see the world projected into your inner dialogue, so does your higher self - she just sees it as if everything has already worked out and you get to choose which movie you will play and project out into your life.

I know, this is a lot to take in. I mean, first it was all this ego stuff and now I'm telling you that if you want to change your life, you have to pretend like it's already happened. Yeah, that sounds about right. But listening to your higher self isn't as easy as listening to your ego because frankly, we're taught to only trust what we know. We lose that sense of wonder and curiosity that we had as kids as soon as we're adults living in the "real word". And in order for your higher self to get through to you, it uses nudges, signs, and synchronicities to guide you to the things that really light you up. And unlike your ego, your higher-self wants you to succeed, in everything.

Think about it like this, if you're climbing up a mountain that you've never climbed before and you're trying to do it all by yourself by ignoring your higher self and her pleading nudges, you're basically throwing your trail map to the wind and just hoping for the best. You see, your higher self is your tour guide. She knows where the glistening fresh drinking water is. Where the best campsites are. Where the most magical waterfalls are. And how to avoid a family of ravenous mountain lions. She knows the mountain like the back of her hand and if you follow her, she'll get you to the top a whole hell of a lot faster. And probably with a lot less cuts and bruises too. But how can you follow something that you can't actually see? I mean, it's not like your higher self is standing in front of you waving excitedly in your face like a kid on their first day of school. This is when faith comes in. Or belief, or trust or whatever you want to call it.

You follow your higher self by feel. Yes, that's right. You literally feel your way to your best life with your higher self as your guide. You do this by trusting that your higher self is your ride or die. That she's there protecting you, guarding you and moving you forward into a life bigger than your wildest dreams. And all you have to do is trust her.

Sounds pretty straight forward. Simple even. Trust, feel, believe. Easy peasy! But uh, if it's so easy, why isn't everyone doing it? Why aren't people dancing around in their best lives, living it up like there's no tomorrow, or galloping through a field of poppies? Well, human beings like to make things complicated. We are skeptical of things that appear too easy, too simple. Why? I honestly don't know.

What I do know is that as human beings we also feel a range of emotions. But most of these emotions are stuffed down. Or I should say, the "bad" emotions are shoved so far down into our bodies that they eventually become heavy, rock-like almost. Sometimes these "rocks" build walls which can feel like permanent structures living inside of you. We carry these heavy, "bad" emotions around with us in a suitcase labeled "baggage" for our entire lives. Until we decide to release them of course.

What do feelings have to do with your higher self anyway? Well, not only are they the subject everyone loves to avoid, they are also one of the many ways your higher self gets your attention and communicates with you. It's kind of like your higher self is saying,

"Hey! I'm talking to you! Go this way instead. It might be different than what you expected but I promise, it's way more fun."

If you listen closely enough, you'll hear it.

Your feelings let you know when you are in alignment or out of alignment. And no, I don't mean your aching back. I mean in alignment with your higher self, ya know, the version of you that will help you go up any mountain you're climbing in a way that makes it feel like you're on an all-expenses paid tour.

"Negative" feelings such as, fear, anger, frustration, and unfulfillment are tell-tale signs that you are not in alignment. "Positive" feelings such as, fulfillment, happiness, curiosity, excitement, and gratitude are signs that you are. When you feel good, you're on the right path. When you don't feel good, something is out of alignment. Simply put, you're in alignment when you are thinking, feeling, speaking, and acting as the version of you who has done whatever it is you want to do, even when what you want to do takes you out of your comfort zone. Spoiler alert, your higher self will always kick you out of your comfort zone because growth happens outside of it. Think of your feelings and emotions as the filter your higher self uses to tell you if what you believe is truth or a construct of your ego mind. Meaning the belief was not yours to begin with.

After the initial shock of all this information, this is starting to sound really amazing right? You finally have a little cheerleader on your shoulder cheering you on and pushing you forward and you even have a roadmap that tells you what's working and what's not. It's like having a cheat sheet to the test in your back pocket! But the thing is, listening to your intuition can be really challenging. Simply because your intuition will always push you to do things that make you uncomfortable. Which means, yes, your ego pops up out of nowhere to tell you to take a deep dive back into your comfort zone. Guess which voice is louder. Ding, ding, ding - your ego.

The question now becomes about how you step into your higher self, or the version of yourself who has the life that you want knowing that your ego will try to derail your efforts? The answer is actually simpler than you might think and it comes down to do two things, awareness, and asking yourself questions. That's it. Become aware of when your ego is showing up, then ask yourself questions to filter if what your ego is saying or doing fits with your higher self.

The thing is, once you become aware of your ego she loses her power over you. She is no longer running your life on autopilot. You catch her red handed in the act and once you do, you ask questions to get a solution to the problem your ego is so fixated on.

This can be a really scary place for your ego and at first you may notice her throwing a bit of a temper tantrum. Okay, a really big, wailing, legs, hands and feet in the air, face turning crimson red, embarrassing, everyone is looking at you in the grocery store, type of tantrum. You see, your ego has run the show for years and until now she was the star, she was the literal filter you used to make all of your decisions. Once you choose to step into your higher self you then make your higher self the filter in which you live your life and make your decisions. And not only that but, when you step out of your ego and into your higher self, you're going to see things differently. And I don't just mean a few things, I mean everything. You'll pass a flower on your way to work and realize you've never seen it before. You'll look at your backyard and feel more gratitude for it than you ever have before and not because it has changed, but because you've changed.

This is when you can notice life feeling a little out of balance. I want to remind you that these changes don't happen overnight. You will not go to sleep and wake up the next morning a bright, shiny, new person. There is an adjustment period for your mind and body. I'm going to take a deep, deep dive into this in the next chapter but this is important to remember. Your ego may even have you believe that what you're doing isn't working. This is why it is so important to really step into your higher self and use her as the filter in which you make decisions, act, think, feel, and speak because once you do that, your external circumstances can change all they want, but your inner world and state of being will be unchanged.

Your Ego, The Child

Much like a child, when you make any kind of change, no matter how seemingly insignificant, it begins to throw a temper tantrum of emotions and feelings that smack you in the face so hard you might just stop in your tracks. These temper tantrums show up as fear-based thoughts, overthinking, second guessing, thinking of the worst-case scenario, reasons you shouldn't do what you're doing, and it will even bring up old habits. Such as drowning out the fear with alcohol, ignoring the thoughts, running away, or procrastinating. Needless to say, my ego throws everything at me at once. In a big giant ball of swirling stinky excuses, reasons, and nasty thoughts.

The key to all of this is awareness. That's the first step after all. Becoming aware of when your ego pops in to ruin the party. Recognizing what thoughts come up and when, and most of all recognizing that they are coming up from fear. Because to your ego, change threatens you on a primal level. Remember, your ego is just trying to keep you alive and if it can't put your thoughts or actions into a box or folder that's similar to something else, it's going to be afraid for its life.

Once you recognize that your ego is speaking up, use the other techniques in this book to dismantle the fears, demolish the beliefs, and calm your mind enough to begin to see past the giant wall that your ego is putting up in your mind. Then begin to trust that whatever path you are being taken on is the right path for you. Trust that there are lessons there that need to be learned. There are things you have to overcome first that will help you get what you want. You have to learn how to walk before you can run.

How to Tap into Your Higher Self

Get Clear on What You Want:

Notice I didn't say, write a big giant list of what you don't want. Focus on what you do want. Here's the thing, most of the time when you ask someone what they want, they'll tell you everything they don't want. But if you want to tap into your higher self, you're going to have to use your subconscious mind to help you. And your subconscious mind doesn't process negatives such as can't and don't.

So, what do you want? What do you want your life to look like? What would you be doing if you had a magic wand that could give you everything you desire? How would your life look if all your fears and limiting beliefs were gone? More importantly, what do you want your life to FEEL like?

Write that all down in a notebook and write them as, "I now have..." or, "I have [insert what you want]".

Write Down the Details of That Version of You:

Think about how that version of you would think. How that version of you would show up in the world. The beliefs that you would have. The daily habits you would have. How she feels. What are her values? Get very clear on this because the more detail you have, the easier it will be for you to embody the characteristics, thoughts, and behaviors of your higher self.

Write them in a notebook and again, use present tense, "I am [blank]".

Visualize What You Are Doing, How You Are Feeling and What You Are Thinking:

To see your desired manifestations in your physical reality, you must first see it in your mind. This is also a way to get your subconscious mind involved because it thinks in images and pictures and remember, your subconscious mind is what is connected to the Universe, telling it exactly what to bring into your life.

Get quiet and ask yourself what you want your life to look like - what would you be doing? What would you be feeling? Where would you be going? Who would you be with? See yourself in your mind doing, being, having, and feeling all of things. The best way for the subconscious mind to latch onto this is to see yourself as a third person. Like you're looking into a crystal ball watching yourself live out your best life.

I understand that visualizing isn't easy for everyone so if you find you're unable to visualize or see yourself doing, feeling, and having everything you want, tap into the feelings you want. How would you feel if you had your dream life? What will these external things you're chasing make you feel? Yes, it really is all about the feelings. Do this while sitting quietly every single day for 10 minutes.

Align Your Actions with Your Vision:

If you see yourself working 10 hours a month, speaking on stages, owning 10 dogs and living it up with your BFF, don't spend your time grinding and hustling 80-hour work weeks, avoiding putting yourself out there, and fighting with your best friend.

Align your actions with your vision by doing the things that will get you closer to the version of yourself you visualized. Do this in small steps and really take note of the type of actions you are taking on a daily basis. Before you say yes or no to something, ask yourself if that task is in alignment with who you want to be. If it is, great, if not, ask yourself what action you need to take to be in alignment.

"Your feelings are the filter your higher self uses to let you know if what you believe is truth or simply a construct of your ego mind."

CHAPTER 14

THERE IS CLARITY IN CHAOS

Picture this; you're a young child again, cuddled up in your warm plush covers, surrounded by your favorite stuffed animals. There's an owl hooting right outside your window while the tree in your backyard casts a long, gangly shadow across your bed and walls. Your stomach rumbles and you realize the only thing that will cure the craving in your belly is a cup of warm milk and a chocolate chip cookie. You pull back the covers and let your feet slide to the floor. Before your feet touch the carpet, you look down and to your horror, you see something slither out from underneath your bed!

Don't worry, you didn't take a wrong left turn and end up smack dab in the middle of a Steven King novel. The scary part is almost over. All you have to do is just take a closer look and shine a light on that slimy slithering beast under your bed, so that you can see it for what it actually is. An old sweater, maybe a pair of mismatched shoe laces, or even a half-eaten slice of cheese pizza.

You see, the only power those monsters had over you was the idea that they were real. And once you realized they weren't, they slinked back to their respective drawers and closet spaces. I use this analogy because I think we can all relate to it and although you're an adult now, these fears still come up in everyday life. At first glance these things appear scary, chaotic even. But once you shine a light on them, you're able to see them for what they truly are.

I'm talking about the times when you feel like you're doing everything right. You're meditating daily, you're journaling, you're doing your affirmations, you've banished your ego more times than you've listened to it, you're showing up as your higher self, you're listening to your intuition and yet, your life feels like it's falling apart at the seams. You're getting unexpected bills. Your car breaks down. You get bad news out of nowhere. And it all comes crashing down. Or at least it feels that way.

Your ego looks at these times and entices you like a siren back into the depths of your old life. She'll whisper stories in your ear about how easy life used to be. How you'll be so much happier if you just stop doing things that make you uncomfortable. She will use your fear as the fuel to her fire. And if that doesn't work, she'll get loud. Louder than she ever has before. She'll fill your mind with images of an easier time, an easier life, and for a second, you might even believe her.

When life gives you lemons you have two choices; experiment with different lemonade recipes and see which one works the best, or spend hours, months, or even years sitting and staring at the lemons wondering what in the hell to even do with them. Technically there is a third choice. Which would be to yell and scream at the stupid lemons while throwing them at the wall of your house. I don't recommend this but it's an option.

You might be thinking that life would just be so much easier if you didn't have to deal with problems ever again. If everything was just easy for you. Yeah, I've been there. That thought crossed my mind once or twice - or a thousand times. Logically speaking yes, life would be easier if we didn't have polarity - light and dark. But would it be more fun? Would it be more enjoyable?

I used to play video games with my best friend all the time. Literally, all the time! Back then I didn't have the same games she had so I was always so excited when I would get to go over to her house so that we could play together. Well, as you might've guessed, because she had access to these video games all the time and had more time to practice playing them, she was really good at them. Whenever I would play with her, she always won. Literally. Always. Eventually, this got old and it wasn't fun anymore because I knew, no matter what game we played, she would always win. I knew the outcome of the game which took all the fun out of it.

What you may not realize is that the growth is in the unknown. It's in the times when it looks like things aren't working out. When it feels like everything is falling apart. It is in these dark times that if you just took a minute to shine a light, you'd see the lessons, you'd see where you need to improve, where you need to pivot. Sometimes, you need those walls to break down, to fall apart, in order for you to allow more things in. If everything was all rainbows and butterflies, you'd never grow. You'd never learn. You'd never be moving up a level. Frankly, that sounds pretty boring to me.

When I was a kid, I played this Scooby Doo game on my Nintendo 64 (stop it your age is showing...) No matter how many hours I played it I couldn't get past this stupid mummy thing that kept chasing me. And I would get so frustrated, I just wanted to move up to the next level! One day I was so fed up I decided to go onto the Internet and find a cheat code to get past that level.

Lo and behold, it was a lot easier than I thought and boom, I was onto a new level with a new challenge. I spent months sitting in frustration, pushing harder, doing more, throwing the controller around and being angry about not getting past that one level, when all it took was learning a cheat code that allowed me to get past that level in just a few minutes.

When it comes to real life, the cheat codes are in the chaos. I realize how this sounds but seriously, they're in there. They may not be as black and white as the cheat codes you find on the internet but they're there. They show up as feelings, thoughts, beliefs, and words bubbling up and over like tomato soup that you left in the microwave for too long. They are the defaults, the gut reaction, the said without thinking words that cut like a knife.

If you want to heal a wound, you have to see it first. You have to see what you're working with. Chaos is the Universe's way of helping you rip off the band-aid so that you can see where you need to grow and what the lessons are that will help you get to the next level. I went through life for years taping up my wounds with brightly colored band aids with funny little characters on them and smiling faces in hopes that no one would notice the cracks. I fooled myself into thinking I was okay. That it was normal to drink alone almost every night. That it was normal to yell and scream profanities at your significant other. I pretended that it was normal for life to be hard, for me to have to struggle day in and day out. And worst of all, I truly believed I deserved it. I deserved the pain. Sometimes I'd cover it up, other times I intentionally made it worse. Like twisting the knife in a gaping wound.

Oftentimes I'd go in search of the situations that I knew would hurt but I also knew they would give me the validation of not being worthy of love and deserving of pain. This cycle of self-destruction manifested itself as a drinking problem, dating men who didn't love me, believing I needed something outside of myself to make me feel better, settling for jobs that didn't light me up, and allowing my ego to spit and spew poison all over me.

I focused so hard on life's struggles I wasn't able to see anything else. It was like I had a filter over my life and all I could see was the worst of it. Not only that but these default thoughts, feelings, and behaviors kept showing up in my life time and time again because they were trying to show me something. They were trying to help me learn so that I could come out the other side into a new level. And it wasn't until I took a step back and saw the tiny cracks for what they were that I realized I could use them to heal.

This is when you can ask yourself the tough questions, the questions that your ego loves to hate. The questions that inevitably shine a light so brightly that you can't ignore it anymore. And the quicker you lean into the chaos, accept it for what it is, look at it with love and choose to find the lesson in it, the faster you will move through it into a new "level" of your life.

Have you ever been in a room with 18 barking, howling dogs with one dog literally the size of a freaking bear leading the pack, because the UPS guy just had to park right in front of the window? No? Well I have. Your first instinct would be to quiet them all by yelling over them. Maybe clapping or making a noise of some sort, right? In reality, you're just adding more noise to the already unsettling, increasing volume level. When you focus on the problem, and try to fix the problem using the same tactics that created that problem, you'll just create an even bigger problem. It's like trying to fight fire with fire. You're quite literally just creating a bigger fire.

The point I'm trying to make here is this; if you focus on, and put all of your energy into, what's going wrong, i.e. the chaos, you'll never be able to see what's going right. What if losing that job opened the door for your dream job? What if getting your heart stomped on by a lying, cheating boyfriend allowed you to find your soulmate? What if getting 100 "nos" made you appreciate that "yes" that much more?

The fact of the matter is this; you will experience a period of what feels like chaos. A period of challenges that you need to overcome. A dragon to slay if you will. This is just inevitable. But it is this chaos that allows you to advance to a new level. The purpose of a challenge, or chaos or things going wrong, is so that you can grow bigger than them and you will gain the tools necessary to overcome anything and everything that pops up in your life. There is immense beauty in this time of your life, you just have to choose to see it that way and trust that it is happening for your highest good.

I realize this is easier said than done but I want to show you how a simple reframe can make all the problems, or chaos or things going wrong in your life, feel simple, easy and even, dare I say it, fun to overcome.

Think of the word "problem". Notice how that word makes you feel. Take note of the images that come to mind when thinking about the word "problem". Now think about the word "challenge". Again, notice the feelings, thoughts, and images that come up for you when thinking about the word "challenge". Finally, think about the word "opportunity" and notice the thoughts, feelings, and images that come up when you think about that word. I'm going to guess that the word "opportunity" made you feel much more excited and open, like the world is your oyster. I'm also going to guess that the word "problem" brought up some negative images, feelings, and thoughts.

Opportunity, challenge, and problem are all the same thing, they are just looked at through a different lens. But challenge and opportunity feel so much better than problem. Why? Because we've associated a different meaning to what those words mean based on how we look at them and perceive them. None of them have a meaning until you give it one and you will give every single word a meaning based on how you are looking at them and your past meanings.

This is important because chaos, problems, challenges, and opportunities are all necessary for growth. If you want to grow in any way shape or form, you're going to have to go through some growing pains. And if you want to make these growing pains easier to go through, change the words you are using or change the meanings you are giving to them.

At the time that I'm writing this book, my nephew is learning to walk and it's really exciting watching him learn how to do something that is brand new to him. At first, he was a really fast crawler. Like lightning fast. And because walking is new to him, he's slower, he falls a lot more, it's harder and something he's never done before. I wondered if he would favor crawling because he was so good at it but lo and behold, he kept practicing walking. He'd fall, get back up, fall, get back up until eventually, all he did was walk. Then he'd run. Then he'd jump. Then he'd dance. Even though he was going through a season of "chaos", or a season of going through something he was uncomfortable with that he had never done before, he kept going because he knew this was what the next step was.

The goal of this chapter is not to get you to banish all things "bad", chaotic, or scary into the deep dark depths of some invisible pool. It's to get you to recognize that the struggle is there to teach you. It is there to show you what you need to work on, what lessons you still need to learn and how to overcome them. I also want you to start looking at things differently, with a fresh perspective. One that doesn't make you go red with rage or curl into a ball of fear.

This is why learning how to step into your higher self is so important. Because if you look at chaos through your ego lens, it's going to look like a giant brick wall standing in your way. But if you look at it through your higher self, and with the end in mind, it's like going through it with a GPS and yellow signs showing you where the construction is. You might have to go through that construction to get to where you want to go but you'll go through it with a purpose to come out the other side stronger than when you went in.

Chaos Is Making Space on a Universal Level

Chaos doesn't just happen to help you grow and learn the lessons that you need to learn, it's also happening to create space for the things you desire. The things that will help you be your higher self. I like to think that the Universe is playing a game of chess or playing with a puzzle. The Universe will move the pieces of the chess game that will allow you to flourish, help you to grow and succeed. And the pieces that don't fit will be moved out of the way.

These pieces can be jobs, people, situations, beliefs, thoughts, feelings - anything that no longer serves you. The Universe is literally pushing these things out of your life because they were the pieces of your life that no longer fit. They don't work with the new reality you're creating. Remember, if you want a different reality, you have to change the way you think, feel, and act. And when chaos hits or what feels like chaos, this is the Universe's way of making space for you to grow.

Another way to think about this is a plant trying to flourish and grow in a pile of weeds. There are so many weeds the flower can't grow. It tries to plant its roots, it's given plenty of water, fresh air, and sunshine (all external things) but the weeds are just taking it over and the plant is unable to grow the way it needs to. Now remove those weeds and the flower blooms for the whole world to see. This is what the Universe is doing for you. But if you're so stuck holding onto these things that no longer serve you by making excuses for your comfort zone, holding onto your old beliefs, and gripping as hard as you can to your old life, this period of chaos is going to feel like...well, chaos.

Some of the best things that ever happened to me were the most painful breakups, the friendships that ended in fights, and the beliefs that smacked me so hard in the face they left a bruise. If these hadn't happened, I wouldn't be sitting here writing this book, living a life that I could only dream of. Change is a blessing, even the most painful changes have a reason.

Let go, trust that the Universe has a plan and see it from your higher self's perspective. Everything is always working out in your favor. Always. And the more you believe that, the more it will be true for you.

How to Find the Clarity in the Chaos:

1. Lean In:

Chaos is like quicksand, the more you fight it, the quicker it will suck you in and the more you will have to struggle. The natural reaction when things go awry is to avoid it, cover it up, pretend it's not happening or literally run away from it. What you resist persists. This means if you avoid what's going on it's going to happen again and again and again until you learn the lesson.

Lean into the chaos, do the opposite of what your ego is telling you to do, listen to what the situation is trying to tell you, and trust that it will never last forever and the quicker you get out of it what you need to, the quicker you will move up to a bigger level.

2. Reframe, Reframe, Reframe:

Instead of seeing the chaos as a bad thing that is ruining your life or that what you're doing is wrong, see it as a way to grow. To succeed faster. To gain all the tools you need to overcome any challenge that comes your way. A reframe is a choice that can be made on a dime.

3. Ask Yourself Result Based Questions:

What is this situation trying to teach me?

What can I learn from this?

How can I grow from this situation?

What are the tools needed to overcome this obstacle?

How can I reframe what is happening to better serve me?

It's these types of questions that give you the best answers when it feels like everything is falling apart. Remember, if you ask yourself really good questions, you'll get really good answers.

4. Journal:

Journaling it out and physically putting your words to paper can help you see things that you cannot see as clearly in your mind. You can begin to notice your thought patterns and see where your ego is showing up in how you are perceiving what is happening.

5. Practice Gratitude:

I know, I get it. The last thing you want to do is say "thank you" to a situation that is making you want to scream. But gratitude is something that your ego just cannot compete with. When you become grateful for the situation that is going on around you, you immediately shift from,

"Why is this happening **to** me?" to,

"This is happening **for** me."

And when something is happening **for** you, you always have something to gain from it.

6. Throw Some Love at It:

When in doubt, love conquers all. Throw love at yourself for feeling the way you are feeling, throw love at the situation and understand it is happening for you, and throw love at anyone else the situation affects.

7. Stop Drop and Align:

It is in times of chaos that your ego will have you believe that you need to do more, take more massive action, hustle more, grind harder. Doing more will never give you the result you want. When you take action from a place of fear, scarcity or lack, that is the energy you will receive back from the action you took.

Take a step back and get into alignment with your higher self. How would she handle this situation? How would she feel? How would she think? Asking yourself these questions will get you back into alignment with the version of you who sees these situations with the end in mind and knows that everything is working out in your favor. And because of this, any action you do take will be taken out of love and wisdom which means that is what you get back.

8. Trust the Universe

Trust that whatever is happening around you is happening for you on a Universal level. The Universe has the power to bring people into your life that will help you achieve your greatest goals. The Universe also helps you clear the "weeds" - and the way - by helping you release the people, situations, beliefs, thoughts, and actions that no longer serve you.

Sometimes the Universe does this by shining a mirror in your face and asking you to look yourself in the eye and do some massive self-reflection. Other times it's more subtle, and the friends that you no longer need fall away easily and you both mutually fall out of touch. Either way, look for the signs of things falling apart and get very clear on how this could be happening for you and what the Universe is trying to do. Look for the lesson and trust that there is something so much better on the other side.

"There is clarity in chaos. Instead of seeing everything as falling apart, choose to see it as everything that no longer serves you is falling away to make way for the pieces of your best life to fall together."

CHAPTER 15

GROWING PAINS SUCK

The date is March 23, 2003. My eyes are heavy, my body is sore, and I can hear a buzzing inside my head. There's this heaviness on my chest that I'm trying to see so that I can move it off of me but the world is fuzzy. The lights are too bright. Seriously. Someone shut those off! I try to sit up but I can't. I feel like there's a brick tied to my back that's preventing me from moving. I blink a few times and breath in, now realizing I'm in a hospital. My parents are near the end of the bed and there's a nurse standing next to me. And what's this? She's playing a game of chess and using my stomach as the board! This is nonsense, inappropriate behavior for someone who is supposed to be taking care of me! I yell out and tell her to stop. I can see the uneasy smile run across my parent's faces. But apparently this is normal for someone who has just awoke from an 11-hour surgery.

It all comes flooding back to me as I try to close my eyes while nurses shine flashlights in my face and rush me around the long corridor to my new room for the night. I'm just so exhausted but I'm not allowed to sleep just yet. I had just come out of a spinal fusion surgery. My spine is now fitted with brand new shiny metal rods which left a pencil thin scar down the length of my back. My stomach on the other hand is missing a rib and is now decorated with an unsightly red and purple scar from my belly button to a few inches away from my armpit. I knew this was what had to be done for me to live a normal healthy life with a spine that was straight instead of one that curved like an old winding road. But what I didn't expect was what came next. The growing pains, the whole, learning how to live with rods in my back thing. It was going to be like this for the rest of my life. I didn't have a choice.

This was my new normal as my dad always says. I had to learn how to live with a spine that was less than flexible, three scars that made me cringe every time I stepped out of the shower or put on a bathing suit and a life of people asking me what happened. I was in the hospital for 10 days, learning how to live with my new straight back and cut up stomach. I always liked long walks on the beach, but now my time was spent taking slow strolls down the hospital walkways with a nurse clutching my arm and a walker in front of me. It was painful, frustrating, and at times, humiliating. I mean I literally couldn't even wipe my own butt let alone sit up in bed without feeling like my chest and back were being beaten on like a set of drums.

I was lucky though. I healed quickly. I learned how to maneuver my new body, I gained the strength I needed to walk up the stairs on my own, shower, and live with my new...adjustments. I learned how to embrace my scars, I learned how to grow because I had no other choice. As much as I wanted to rip out the rods and go back to my old painful, curved spine, I couldn't. I had to learn how to live with these new tools that I was given.

That's the thing, I knew the alternative was more painful than the season of growth I was going through. I chose this surgery because I knew if I didn't my life would be spent in a stinky, white, plastic back brace with pads that dug painfully into my hips while I slept or simply lived my daily life. Weekly trips to chiropractors that smelled sickly like too much hand sanitizer, and doctors that moved and cracked my body in ways I didn't even know the human body was meant to be moved. Not to mention the x-rays that showed the ever growing "S" curves that made up my spine. And just like a cherry on top, pain that radiated through my back and hips.

That's what growth is. Learning how to live with something new because the alternative is more painful than the growth you're experiencing. Whether that's rods in your back or a new and improved mindset. Growth isn't easy. It isn't rainbows and butterflies. I mean from the last chapter I'm sure you've gathered that. But oftentimes we paint this picture of happy little clouds and bushes. Of how growing is like coming out of a cocoon into a beautiful butterfly. But there are messy bits in the middle that people like to ignore. There's a learning period and a time to figure out your new life.

Growth is hard because you're doing something you've never done before. But that's also why it's so beautiful. *Because* you get to do something you've never done before. You get to experience life in a different way, through a different lens, and that's pretty damn exciting if you ask me. Do you want to know why most people continue to live the same life they've always lived, allowing their ego to control their every move and complaining about where they are at? Because to get to the life you've always wanted, you're going to have to go through growth first. It's a necessary stepping stone to get to where you want to be. And just like stepping a toe outside of your comfort zone, it makes your ego pop in and throw fear and self-sabotage all over the walls of your mind.

Knowing that growth can be a tough lesson to grow through (see what I did there), is there any way to make it easier? Well, what if I told you that you could in fact change your comfort zone, because the only reason growth is hard is because what you are doing is something that is outside of it. I mean, if it was comfortable don't you think it wouldn't be as hard? Changing your comfort zone isn't a big complicated, or even scary, thing, all it takes is a few reframes and you're on your way. Reframing can be done by changing the meaning of the situation or even by changing the context. And as human beings, we give meaning to a lot of things... well, most things. It's just part of being a human, which is why reframing the meaning can be so powerful. The thing is, you get to decide what something means to you. That's just a small sliver of power that you have.

Let's just be honest, you're reading this book in a bubble. And it's all good and gravy while you're reading it but eventually, you're going to have to go back to the real world. Of course, you're going back to the world with new found knowledge and a hell of a lot more awareness for your thoughts, ego, feelings, and actions which can make living life a million times more fun. But you're also going to run into things that are undesired. Negative people, unwanted feelings, people who don't understand what you're talking about, things not going the way you planned - the list goes on. And it's your job now to choose to create a new meaning about all those things. That's the hardest part with all of this. When you learn about changing your mindset, and how your child ego has been driving the car for years, it's exciting, you feel like you have all this power and you do, but then you also want everything to change with you. You still want that instant gratification and to see your environment change along with your shiny new insides.

This is usually when the chaos hits and it feels like everything is falling apart, and as you learned in the previous chapter, that's not the case. My point with all this is, growth is painful, uncomfortable, and oftentimes frustrating because we keep plastering on the same meaning to things even after we've been fitted with a new tool belt. If you truly want to apply everything you've learned in this book to day to day life, you're going to have to drop the old labels and give new meanings to everything you thought you knew.

How to Give New Meaning to Everything in your Life

You're getting ready for a really hot date. You've done your hair, got a new outfit on deck, you're jamming out to today's greatest hits and you're feeling confident as all hell. Three hours before you're supposed to meet your date they call and cancel, saying they're unable to tell you why right now but they're really sorry.

Immediately you start thinking about all the things you did wrong. About all the reasons your date canceled. Maybe they're married, maybe they just aren't that into you. Maybe you're not attractive enough. Your mind spins with fear which inevitably turns to anger. Well they suck, I don't like them that much anyway. They're stupid and ugly. And no one cancels on me like that. What a bunch of BS! You hold these feelings in until a week later when you see your date for the first time. They then tell you that their dog had passed away and they were spending the night at the vet with them when they had called to cancel the date. They were too choked up to say something in the moment and just needed some time to process which is why they hadn't called since.

Insert favorite scenario here. It's not what happened externally that matters, it's what happened internally. Your reaction to the external. You first created a meaning about yourself based on your date's behavior, then decided what it meant about them. Sure, it sucks to feel like you've been ghosted, but wouldn't life be that much more fun if you simply changed the meaning?

Let's try this again. Date calls to cancel. Your response? Okay, no problem! Now I have some extra time to read that book that I've been putting off, or I can have that dinner with my friend that's in town. I don't know about you but reframing the meaning sounds like a lot more fun and enjoyable than huffing and puffing about something you can't control.

When something undesired happens ask yourself,

"What meaning can I give this that makes me feel good?" And guess what? If this date keeps cancelling on you, you get to decide if you will tolerate it or not which teaches you what is okay and what is not.

You can't change the world, you can't control someone else, but you can grab your reframing tool out of your tool belt and use it.

What really are problems?

Growth and problems go hand in hand. It's an inevitable part of growing. Of course, you can throw a reframe at the word "problem" and call it something else but let's take a minute and figure out what problems actually are because you have to deal with them no matter what level you're on.

I want you to try something on for me. Try on the idea that problems are the required lessons of what you want out of life. They're the dual part of life. The necessary polarizing part that makes life interesting. The dark in the light. However, you want to phrase it. But think about it. What if problems arise to teach you something before you get to the good stuff? So that you can enjoy the good bits that much more.

When I was in my early 20's I had my heart broken for the first time. Like really smashed on with a hammer 47 times. It hurt. A lot. But it was one of the best things that could have ever happened to me. It took a few years for me to recognize it because I was so focused on the problem (getting thrown out into the street like a pile of trash – it felt like that anyway) but once I reframed the problem to a lesson, I saw something really incredible. I learned how to value myself. I learned how to set boundaries. I learned how to have a 100-100 relationship with people. Which opened endless doors and opportunities to have high quality relationships. Both platonic and romantic.

Going into an 11-hour surgery at 12 years old taught me that I'm so much more resilient than I ever could have imagined myself to be. I learned how to trust people, how to allow others to help me, how to appreciate life because you never know what tomorrow will bring to the table.

Problems are lessons with a fuzzy picture. Once you turn up the dial on that picture, make it a bit brighter, clearer and more colorful, you're able to fully see what you couldn't before. That you need to learn the lesson that equips you with the tools that will allow you to enjoy the things you want that much more fully.

You have two choices when it comes to growth. You can either complain the whole way there, kicking, scratching, yelling and screaming and trying to grab onto anything and everything you possibly can to make you stay where you are. Or you can choose to take the lessons that the growth is giving you and use those lessons to help you get to where you want to go that much faster.

Recognizing Self-Sabotage and Its Dirty Tricks

As I said, your ego will throw fear and self-sabotage all over the walls of your head as soon as you decide to make a run for some change and growth around here. I'm dedicating an entire chapter on self-sabotage because it can be so devastating so for now, keep these tricks in mind to help you notice when self-sabotage rears its ugly head.

Procrastination:

This is one of the most obvious forms of self-sabotage and it comes in many different forms. From blatantly ignoring that stack of paper work, to making excuses and reasons why you can't do certain things. We spend so much time holding onto our reasons and excuses that we don't even realize that all that time spent arguing could have been used to get things done.

Staying Busy:

Busy is not a badge of honor that you get to wear around the mall and tell everyone about. Being busy means nothing if what you're working on doesn't align with who you want to be. It's an easy trap to fall into because you think you're getting all these things done! Your to-do list is neatly checked off and it feels good. Here's a little reality check, the things that make the biggest splash in our lives are usually the things that pull us out of comfort zones and force us to do something we've never done before.

Blaming/Complaining:

Putting the blame onto someone else is your ego's forte. Your ego can't be wrong because if it was then who would it be?? So, it's everyone else's fault. That's easier to do. You do not have control over people, so putting your life and how it looks into someone else's hands is pretty dangerous. Look, if you want to decide how your life looks, then be 100% responsible for the things you can change and choose to be 100% responsible for how you react to everything that happens.

"Ready" - An Illusion.

We chase this thing, this "ready", because we think it's something we can hold in our hands. "When I feel ready then I will do blank, blank, blank." Let me ask you this, when was the last time you ever felt ready to do anything you've never done before? Ready is an illusion, don't fall for it.

Doing the Same Things and Expecting a Different Result

This is a tricky one I'll admit. It's tough to spot but when you do, it will make a world of difference. You can see this in the relationships you're in, the jobs you take, the behaviors and habits you have, and well, the results you're getting. Frankly, if you're getting the same results over and over and over again, maybe just in a different order, it's probably because you're doing the same things over and over and over again. Take note of automatic habits and behaviors and take stock of if they are actually working or not. You have the tools, you just have to do it.

Get Back Up When Life Kicks You To The Ground

As a kid, my neighbors and I would set up this big obstacle course with different tricks and jumps for us to glide over on our roller blades. My parents' house was right at the top of the hill so we would push off from the front porch and go sailing down the sidewalk, gaining speed, jumping, skidding and flying all the way down for the whole neighborhood to see. I can't tell you how many times I fell and scraped my knees, bloodied my wrists and elbows, and cried in pain while hydrogen peroxide sizzled in my wounds. That's part of life. It knocks you down. It throws you around and spits you out. Sometimes that's falling on concrete, having two serious and dangerous surgeries 10 days apart or getting your heart stomped on by a boy who never really loved you. Your ego will make you believe you should stay down. It will fill your mind with thoughts of fear of it all happening again and again so that you stop trying.

So how do you get back up when life knocks you down? How do you step into the next level that you're being prepared for? You learn the lessons that were presented to you and take the knowledge from them to do something different next time. If you fell while rollerblading because your foot hit a rock, move the rock. Don't keep running into the same rock and then wondering why you keep falling. Learn the lesson. If a boy broke your heart, look for someone with different qualities and values than the first one. Make a list of what you will tolerate and what you won't. Take note of the lessons you can learn from the hard stuff. Your ego can't see them because you can't see lessons from a place of fear. Release the fear and ask yourself, "What do I need to learn from this?" Then listen for what comes up.

Sometimes these lessons aren't made clear until years later. Other times they're right in front of us in the blink of an eye. The goal isn't to always be right or to always know the answer right away, it's to be aware that there's something in this for you to learn. There's something here you can take with you so that you can slay the dragon in the next level of life. If you find yourself thinking you need to do or have something first before you can move forward, that's just your ego talking and she's trying to distract you. Learn from her words, and keep moving forward.

"You could be just one small reframe away from your biggest breakthrough ever."

CHAPTER 16

IF I KNEW THEN WHAT I KNOW NOW...

There I was, squatting in a hole in the middle of the woods. I could hear the birds chirping, every stick breaking and the sun shone like a halo of light over my head. I had hiked for at least a thousand miles by now (in reality it was closer to just a few miles) and I could feel the blisters forming on the backs of my legs and feet. There was a dull ache in my back and shoulders from my backpack and an angry red scrape that covered my right upper hip. I had slept in tents with rocks for pillows, helped put the food in the trees so the bears wouldn't get to it, and bathed in the most beautiful crystal-clear lake I had ever seen.

I was on one of those adventure trips for teenagers that was put on by a local club. My friend at the time had wanted to try it and my 15-year-old self thought, what the hell? What do I have to lose? There were 6 of us. Including two adult counselors that were to take us safely through the woods of the Porcupine Mountains in Michigan and bring us back home. Because it was the woods and all, there were no showers, no bathrooms, no places to sleep so we had to carry everything with us on our backs like pack mules. If you didn't want to carry it, don't bring it. We also didn't have phones or music or podcasts to listen to. We were all left to our own thoughts swirling around inside our own heads. The only sounds available to drown out the, "What in the actual f*ck did I get myself into?" was the rustling of the trees, the crackling branches and the feet shuffling as we all walked in silence in a line through the woods.

As much as we all wished someone would walk into poison ivy so that we could run to the bus and go home early, we never gave up, we never stopped moving forward and we kept our trust in our counselors. That's not to say that I didn't have many thoughts of turning back, falling and refusing to get up, or wishing I was anywhere but squatting in the middle of the woods behind a bush that barely covered my lower half. I decided I had no other choice but to stay committed to my goal. Committed to getting through this backpacking trip with stories that I would someday put in a book even if I had to grit my teeth the whole way there.

You would think that an adventurous little soul like myself would have been bungee jumping off bridges in Australia, cascading down snow covered mountains in Colorado, and swimming with sharks in the Great Barrier Reef by the time I was in my mid 20's. But you'd be sadly mistaken.

In my younger years I would get glimpses of her, the person I was meant to be. The one who just went for it, tried without fear of failure, took those big leaps of faith with a smile. She popped up quite often back then but as I got older, she started to fade more and more. And as the years went on, the small glimpses I used to have of her had disappeared altogether.

Oftentimes I look back on the adventures I took back in the day, like jumping off a 40 foot rock for a boy, backpacking in the wilderness, flying 12 hours to Australia for a family trip, going on a blind date for the first time and I think to myself, "If I knew then what I know now, I never would've done it..blah..blah..blah." That's the thing with aged knowledge. It lets your ego in. And allows her to take back the helm of your ship of adventure.

The "think of the consequences" thinking is what buried my love for new things, my curious mind, and left me afraid to leave my couch in fear of the world. If I knew back then what I know now I never would have lived the amazing life I chose for myself. I never would have experienced the world in that way.

Take a look at the way a child sees the world. With fresh eyes. Everything is an adventure. Everything is new and exciting. And they go into these new things with a wide-open mind ready to learn what it all means. They're not afraid, they're not thinking about the "consequences", they're not letting their fear of the unknown dictate what their life is going to look like. They just go for it and take the lessons they need to take from the outcome. Good or bad.

Of course, as adults we have the responsibility and knowledge of consequences and being responsible for our own actions but we forget what it's like to let our curiosity run and play for a little while. We forget what it's like to get out of our heads and let our dreams take us somewhere again. We're so afraid to make a mistake that we let it paralyze us from taking any action at all. Guess what, if you knew then what you know now you probably wouldn't have had as much fun, you probably wouldn't have learned as much, you probably wouldn't be where you are today, good or bad.

Every mistake, every failure, every set-back is what got you here today. It's what shaped you. Molded you like clay. This is one of the most challenging lessons to learn because to your ego, if life isn't all rainbows and butterflies then something is wrong. If you're not safely packed into your comfort zone with your seat belt fastened, fear sets in like smog that clouds your head and fills your lungs. But you need to remember this, you wouldn't appreciate the sun if you didn't see the stars. You wouldn't appreciate life if you didn't know its opposite. The game of life is filled with ebbs and flows that you need to ride through.

Don't let your ego take over and tell you anything different. Because if you knew then what you know now, you wouldn't have the stories that could help thousands. You wouldn't have the experience to get through what life throws at you. You wouldn't have the tools needed to get to the next level. Trust that what was dealt to you was dealt to you for a reason. A big one. One that has the power to help others. And even to help yourself.

Your Past Doesn't Determine Your Future

In this chapter, I've talked a lot about the past. How often were you more adventurous in your past than you are now and when you look back at those times you question if you had a do-over, would you do it differently? Because what you know now is so much different than what you knew back then. So often you use the past to determine what your future will look like. You use a past time to determine what a future time will hold for you.

Time is one of those things that no one really understands completely. It's a human construct meaning someone created it and decided there were 24 hours in a day, 168 hours in a week,

730 hours in a month, and 8,760 hours in a year. Time is a non-renewable resource meaning we can't get it back once it's gone. You can't make more of it, you can't touch it, you can't even really see it, only a representation of it on a calendar or a clock. And yet, we construct our entire life around it. We allow it to determine what lies ahead for us simply based on what happened to you in the past. But the thing is, your past doesn't determine your future. Your present thoughts, feelings, beliefs, and actions do.

Your ego will have you believe that if it happened in the past, there's a 100% chance it will happen again. It's a survival mechanism and while it does work for many things such as avoiding getting soaked in the rain, remembering to bring a map so that you don't get lost, or avoiding people who've hurt you, it's flawed in many other ways. It will hold you back from doing something different simply because your ego believes the outcome is not worth the risk of not knowing. It'll keep you in the same jobs, with the same friends, doing the same things all because your ego can determine what will happen next based on the past. It's like walking on a mountain covered in fog. You can't see 5 inches in front of you which scares your ego. So you stop and turn back around. Little did you know there was a rainbow on the other side. Using the past to determine your future will only lead you to getting the same result. Over and over again. It's when you step into your higher self that you rise above the fog.

It's like playing a game of chess against the Universe and always making the same three moves. The Universe is just following your lead. That's the thing with experience and knowledge. With more of it, you are better equipped to make new decisions and have new thoughts which give you new results. The fact of the matter is, using your past to determine your future is the only surefire way to get the same results you've always gotten. If you want to get new results, as I'm sure you do if you're reading this book, then you're going to need to put a heavier focus on what you're thinking right here and right now and the actions you're taking in the moment. Because it's these moments that determine your next few moments and so on and so forth through all of time.

Your Focus Will Get You Through The Fog

There's nothing quite as terrifying as hanging off the ledge of a 40-foot boulder. The people on the ground look like ants. Your feet are slipping on the small tumbling stones. Your legs are shaking from the intense fear of falling and you're trying to hold yourself steady as you peer through your hair that's falling in your eyes because your helmet is too big. Your mind is racing and going into overdrive thinking of all the things that could go wrong. For a second, you forget you have all the tools you need to climb down this boulder. To overcome this obstacle. And as you give into your trust instead of your fear, you lean back into your climbing harness and start to repel down the boulder. One foot at a time. Slowly but surely your feet reach the bottom.

The unknown is scary. It's a long winding road leading to, well you don't know really. You're hoping it leads to the outcome you want, which is easy to do when you have a clear path laid out in front of you. You can see each step outlined with exactly what it will entail. Simple. Easy. But that's not how life works. That's not how this goes. What it usually looks like is deciding you want something and then being so consumed by how to get there it can feel like you're walking through the thickest fog you've ever seen. You can't see the path and you can't see the end and that's terrifying. So, your ego pulls in the past to help you. To put all your focus on what's happened before to determine what will happen in your future.

That's the thing with focus. It expands. If you focus on not knowing, that's what you will see more of. If you focus on how far away your destination is, that's what you will continue to feel. What I'm asking you to do is to put your focus on trust. Focus on putting one foot in front of the other and trust in knowing that if an obstacle arises, which let's face it, it will, you have all the tools you need to overcome it. And you get these tools from taking lessons from the past instead of putting all your energy into trying to change it.

"If you let your past design your future, you will keep repeating the same painful patterns. If you let your present design your future, you will get more of what you truly want."

CHAPTER 17

FINDING THE COMFORTABLE IN THE UNCOMFORTABLE

While writing this book I am training for a 10k with the final goal of running a full blown, 26.2 mile, marathon. The thing is, I've never run more than 3.1 miles. And by run, I mean, running for a minute or two before standing in the middle of the race bent over with my hands on my knees panting like a dog in labor. Seriously. Running is not something I just fell into. I wasn't on my high school's track team or cross-country team. I don't just run for shits and giggles. And frankly, it's not even something I've ever been good at.

So why am I even doing it? Why would I even want to put myself through something like this?

Because it's uncomfortable.

I spent a lot of my life running from discomfort. Running from things that scared me. Oh the irony. And again, not literally running otherwise I might be more prepared for this adventure I am taking myself on.

Running a marathon scares me. Like a lot. Running any distance further than 1 mile scares me but I'm doing it anyway. The thing is, I've always wanted to be a runner. I'd watch people jogging past me while I walked my dog and it just seemed so effortless for them. I'd watch people run marathons and think how amazing they are. I just wanted to be a runner like them. I wanted to be able to glide on the pavement with the ease and grace of a gazelle. Instead I ended up looking like a herd of newborn elephants clomping my way down the street. We all start somewhere. But no matter how many times I started, I always gave up. Every single time.

I would try running for a few days, sometimes even weeks, and then I'd give up because it was "just too hard". I allowed the discomfort of the unknown and the belief that I couldn't do it because I had never been able to do it to dictate what was possible for me. As much as I loved how the wind felt on my face and the pavement beneath my feet, I couldn't help but wonder when it would be over. When would I be able to stop? When would the discomfort go away?

Avoiding uncomfortable things is kind of part of the gig of being human. Not taking that promotion because it means more responsibility. Avoiding your cute neighbor that you really want to ask out but are too worried about what they will say. Not chasing your dream because you just don't know if it's possible. It's all uncomfortable. It's all scary. It's all just a story that you've made up so big and bright in your mind that it feels real. It feels like it has already happened. So, you avoid it. And you do it to avoid the discomfort and the uncomfortable outcomes that you *think* will happen.

It's in these moments that your ego thrives. She shines brighter than any star in the night sky and guides you not so gently back into your comfort zone. And without the awareness of this happening, this is where you will stay. This is the very box that you will view life from. The thing is, you can get out of this box at any time. It's your choice. But doing so will require you to do something that you've never done before. Which means, getting uncomfortable.

Here's the thing, something is in your uncomfortable box because you put it there. And over the years you put that box higher and higher on the shelf and allowed it to collect dust and cobwebs. More and more boxes of "discomfort" are also placed up there, eventually stacking one on top of another until your shelves are full. Every once in a while, a circumstance comes along and pulls one box down and forces you to confront it. Such as a promotion, an inheritance, a new job, a new lover, getting fired, going through a break up. Soon enough that initial circumstance begins getting comfortable again and anything outside of that comfort zone is once again placed in a box and put on the shelf.

Finding the "comfortable" in the discomfort is like building a muscle. It's going to take consistency, commitment, discipline and of course, a habit to really make it stick. Getting pushed into discomfort by a circumstance is like going to the gym with the New Year's Resolution crowd. The novelty eventually wears off and you're back doing what you were doing, wishing and hoping that you could have something different. The only way to really make it stick is by consciously doing the thing that is outside of your comfort zone and doing it again and again and again.

The thing is, there's this fear that the discomfort will last forever. You're so focused on being in the middle of the discomfort that you're just waiting, wishing and hoping for it to be over. Anytime now. You forget that the only constant in life is CHANGE. Nothing lasts forever because things are always changing. This is one of the biggest lessons I learned when I began running. The time will not go faster, it will not get easier if my sole focus is on how much longer I have to go until I can just be done. And really, how much fun is that? Why would you go through life wishing for parts to be over when you could choose to find the hidden gems that nobody's willing to dig for?

What's in it for me?

We love to know the benefits of something. What we can get out of it. Especially if it's something challenging or difficult. This is easier to evaluate with things you can physically see but it can also work on things you cannot see such as taking the leap into discomfort. If you don't know what you can get out of it or even see the value in it, why would you do it? So, what's in it for you? What can you really gain from following the road of discomfort?

For starters you cannot control every little detail of your life. And if you could, that would be quite boring. This means that there will be things outside of your control. Something will get thrown at you, you may get knocked off your path a bit and this new thing will probably create some discomfort. By choosing to seek discomfort in everyday life, you will be better prepared for when life throws you a curveball. And you might even be able to see the lessons in it.

The doors of opportunity swing wide open in your favor. How many times have you said you wanted something - a new job, a new home, whatever - and poof, there it is, staring you right in the face but to get it requires a bit of discomfort. Like pitching yourself to a new boss, moving to a new neighborhood, or running 20 miles down a long ass stretch of road that never seems to want to end. So, you pass it up and keep looking for the opportunity to come in again but this time, come in a way that is in your comfort zone. It doesn't happen and you wonder what you did wrong. Why things aren't working out for you. There is no shortage of opportunities in this world. In fact, there are millions coming at you constantly but they just might not be wrapped up in the wrapping paper you thought they would be. They also might, and probably will, require you to get out of your comfort zone in some way. Your ego might squeal with fear, but you don't have to. And by practicing finding comfort in the discomfort, you will see just how many opportunities there are out there that were made for you.

Discomfort forces you to grow and pushes you to find fulfillment and happiness. If you're comfortable all the time and only doing the things that are easy day in and day out, are you really happy? Are you really fulfilled? I can't give you that answer but chances are, you are reading this book because you want more out of life. You want to change; you want something different and you want to live a fulfilling and happy life. Well guess what, that is going to require you getting out of your comfort zone. When you are comfortable with where you are, you are not growing or looking for new ways to grow and learn. This creates dissatisfaction in your life.

It's time like these when you hear people going through a midlife crisis. Because they're not chasing growth, they're not looking to do the thing that others refuse to do. Another way to think about it is this - if you're feeling unfulfilled where you are, the only way up is through discomfort. Once you're in discomfort you have two options, go through it to the other side while taking the lessons with you or go back to the unfilling comfort zone. Your discomfort will push you forward into new, bigger and better things which expand your mind, build your confidence and self-integrity and make you happier.

How to find the Comfort in the Discomfort

Change the Meaning

Your ego is like one big master label maker for everything in your life. It plasters your mind's walls with meanings for your failures, your successes, what your husband or wife said to you this morning, why your dog is looking at you. Everything *has* to have a meaning. But your ego takes it one step further. Every meaning she gives is a meaning about you. About who you are on an identity level.

Which is why if a "meaning" is created around a circumstance that threatens your identity in any way, your ego does everything in its power to self-sabotage the hell out of it.

If someone unsubscribes from my email list that means they hate me.

If that guy I'm in love with cheats on me and stomps all over my heart that means I'm not loveable.

If I don't run a mile in less than 8 minutes then I suck at running.

Really?

That's just your ego trying to make a meaning out of nothing because you see, nothing in life inherently has a meaning besides the one we give it. Which means you can literally change the meaning of the discomfort to mean something that empowers you, pushes you forward, and magnetizes your desires to you. It's just an act of awareness and telling your ego to go play somewhere else.

Focus on your Outcome but be Grateful for the Journey

When I'm running, one of the ways I can make it feel like I've been running through the desert for days without water when it's only been 30 seconds is by focusing on how much further I have left to go. When I sit and moan about how slowly the time is going and all I can see is that stupid red light mocking me with numbers that can't possibly be right, running feels so much harder than it needs to be. And this applies to any type of discomfort that life inevitably throws at you. How do you get through the discomfort? One step at a time.

You can see the outcome to know where you're going but in the moment, feel grateful for the journey. There is always something to be grateful for in every moment. Open your eyes to it and you'll be surprised what you're able to see.

Find the Lessons

Some of the greatest lessons ever learned are from failures. Failing is also one of the most uncomfortable things that can happen to us. No one likes it. Except those that understand what it's all about. Simply put, you're not learning a whole lot by staying in your comfort zone. Actually, you're just relearning the same lesson over and over and over again until you step out of the loop. The faster you find the lesson in the discomfort, the faster you can learn it and move forward with your life.

Two of the most powerful questions you can ask yourself while in the midst of something uncomfortable is, "What is this trying to teach me?" and, "What is the lesson I can learn from this?" The key to getting answers to these questions is to look past your ego and allow your higher self to speak. Meditation or simply sitting quietly can really help with this.

Release it to the Universe

Sometimes just the act of releasing and having full trust that your higher self, the Universe, Source, is taking care of whatever is happening is enough to help you find the comfort you need. Releasing your discomfort to the Universe doesn't mean giving yourself permission to bury your head in the sand and forget all your worries and your cares. It's about trusting that you are a co-creator of your life with the Universe and it's now your job to listen to what comes through you from Source. It's like trying to get through a maze while your best friend has their drone flying over the top of it. They can see things you can't see and it's your job to listen to the directions they're giving you.

Questions to ask yourself when you're going through a season of growth and discomfort:

- What about this is making me feel uncomfortable?
- How can I make this more comfortable for me? Growth doesn't come from avoidance but from finding the comfort in something that isn't comfortable for you yet.
- How can I make this more fun?
- Can I choose to view the discomfort with excitement because that means I'm growing?
- If I changed the meaning of this discomfort would it change how I feel about it?

"Learn to turn losses into lessons and failures into experiments."

CHAPTER 18

CHUTES AND LADDERS

I lived in a small town growing up at the top of a big hill that my brother and I used to fly down on our bikes and rollerblades with our arms behind our backs, hooting and hollering the whole way. I was lucky enough that when we moved into our new house there were a lot of kids for me to play with because who wants to play with their older brother all the time anyway? More like, what older brother wants their little sister cramping their style all day long? Especially because he is five years older than me and I had a major crush on all his friends. Back then, I had no game. During the summer months all my friends would come over to my parent's house and we'd sit on their shaded back porch scribbling boys' names on paper, playing in a blow-up pool filled with bubbles, and oftentimes playing board games. Because back then we didn't have cell phones to entertain us.

One day my friend brought over a game called Chutes and Ladders. 90's kids, you know what I'm talking about. The premise of the game is irrelevant and to be honest, I don't really remember much about it at all but what I do remember is the game board itself which was filled with well, chutes and ladders. Sometimes you'd get lucky and be able to take a ladder up the board pretty high and you'd be almost at the finish line. You were so close you could taste victory. But then you'd get unlucky and boom - down the big winding chute you'd go almost all the way back down to where you first started. There was no real strategy to the game. It was all just luck of the draw. We all knew it was just a game so we'd laugh it off, get bored after a few times playing it through, then proceed to go make sandcastles for the ants in the sandbox or tie up blankets for hammocks in the wooden fort my dad and grandpa built.

That's kind of what life and this whole personal growth thing is like. One day you're walking around going through the motions and then boom, someone shows you a different way of doing things which leads you to taking some "ladders" and moving so close to where you want to be you are ready to take out your wallet and buy a piece of property, when the next minute you can feel yourself sliding back down to what feels like just inches away from where you first began. It can feel frustrating, irritating, and downright aggravating. Sometimes this happens because of uncontrollable circumstances - other times it's your ego playing games. And the game your ego likes to play is called self-sabotage.

Self-sabotage is one of those things that can show up in your life in many different packages and oftentimes these packages are very well hidden. I mean you can see the goal, you can taste it, you can feel it, you're right there and then boom, back down you go in one fell swoop. The secret to combating and overcoming self-sabotage, and the game your ego likes to play in your life, is by first recognizing it and understanding where it's popping up in your life.

Focusing on "What if" Scenarios

You've been working your butt off trying to get the new promotion at work. You have noticed your boss giving you bigger projects and you can feel the promotion coming. The night before the big pitch, as you toss and turn in bed, you're going over every single scenario that could possibly happen. What if they don't like me? What if I can't handle it? What if I'm not right for the job? What if the other employees hate me? What if there's someone else more deserving of it?

Thinking this way puts you off your game and makes you nervous the next day. The fact of the matter is, where you put your focus is what expands. So why would you place any focus on what might happen and not put your focus on what you want to happen. If you're going to play the "what if" game at least rig it in your favor.

Indecision

You've given yourself three options: stay where you are, move to Florida, or move to California. You spend weeks, or even months pondering over the pros and cons of each. And yet, the plane tickets have yet to be booked, the house has yet to be bought, and the life you could have isn't being lived. You cannot move forward with a plan when you're stuck in indecision. Trust that whatever decision you make will either give you a lesson that you needed to learn or the outcome you wanted but either way, you will get something and you will be able to move forward knowing that at least you did something.

Comparison

One sure fire way to keep yourself stuck exactly where you are even though you spend most of your afternoon breaks daydreaming about the life you want to live is to compare yourself to someone else. And with social media, this is easier than ever. You are exactly where you need to be in this moment and the more quickly you adopt that belief, the more quickly your life will change for the better. The quickest way up the mountain is by taking one step at a time on your own path. If you are spending all of your time looking around at what everyone else is doing, you will get nowhere fast.

Letting the World Dictate what's Possible for You

If you can think it, feel it, see it, it's possible for you. Period. But just because you've changed, you've grown, doesn't mean the world is going to change with you. Expecting the world to change with you is like expecting the rest of the house to change colors automatically after painting one room. There are going to be circumstances, people, places, and things that don't align with your vision and where you're going. It doesn't matter. And allowing someone else to tell you what's possible or how to live your life is another form of self-sabotage. Because when you allow the world to tell you what's possible, you let your power and your dreams slip through your fingers and land in someone else's hands.

P.S. You're Giving Yourself Rope Burn

Throughout our entire lives we create ties to people. Whether this be through a similar trauma or simply remembering a stranger on the street that smiled kindly at us. Every single day you create these ties to the world around us. Some of these ties make us feel really good and others fester like old sores that never quite seem to go away or heal. That's the thing about your subconscious mind. It remembers everything. Literally, everything. Which is why if someone cuts us off in traffic and we blow up in a fit of rage it's because we are remembering the 15 other people who did that to us over the course of our lifetime.

Sometimes holding onto memories can be helpful. They can make you feel a certain way, bring forth a feeling of joy or happiness. They can even help you manifest and get into the feelings of already having what you want. But other times they can be painful and make you feel like you're dragging a giant brick through a desert. These are the ties that you need to let go of because frankly, they're giving you rope burn from holding onto them so tightly. We hold onto these ties because well, our ego wants to be right. Our ego wants and needs that validation. If you're truly ready to live that big life, it's time to let go.

What I'm about to share with you is something I've talked about before but it is one of the most powerful ways to release the rope, forgive your past, and move forward. It's called Ho'oponopono and it is a Hawaiian forgiveness prayer. Just to be clear, forgiveness is not about the other person. It's not about letting them off the hook. It's about releasing yourself from the ties that you are dragging around with you every single day. Forgiveness is for you and only you.

The prayer is simple and goes like this, "I am sorry, please forgive me, thank you, I love you". I've also heard it said this way, "I am sorry, I forgive you, thank you, I love you". Pick the version that resonates with you the most. This is chanted over and over again until you feel release.

At first glance it may appear that you are saying these things to another person but the way I think of it is this; you are apologizing to yourself for holding onto this baggage that wasn't yours to keep, you are asking for forgiveness from yourself, you are showing gratitude and love to yourself for making the choice to let the past go as well as thanking the past for the lessons it brought to you.

Ho'oponopono can be used in a mediation or simply said to yourself or in your head. The best way to use it is to make it a daily practice to forgive the ties we create every single day and release them so that we can go into the next day cleared of the day before. Remember, holding onto a grudge and pain from the past is like drinking poison and expecting it to hurt the other person. You're only hurting yourself.

Identifying Secondary Gain

One of the most frustrating things about self-sabotaging is learning that you may be benefiting from it in some way shape or form. Even if that benefit is subconscious. Which it usually is. Take the example of someone who smokes. Maybe they hate the taste of cigarettes but whenever they smoke, they feel less stressed, more relaxed. Okay. What about scrolling on social media? Scrolling on social media can make you think about something else even if just for a little while. You're thrust into someone else's life which gives you reprieve from your own.

The idea here is to begin to identify if you are benefiting from the behavior or habit because chances are, you are probably getting something out of it otherwise you wouldn't continue to do it. Then, replace what you are getting with something else. If you feel relaxed when you smoke, what's another way to feel relaxed just as quickly? Ask yourself questions until you find an answer that can help you eliminate the benefits you are receiving. Another way to eliminate secondary gain is to ask yourself what the intention is behind the behavior or habit. Once you get clear on the intention, again, you can find something else to fulfill that benefit.

The Secret to Overcoming Self-sabotage

You can either climb up the mountain or you can repel down it but you can't do both at the same time. Or more commonly stated, you can fight for your limitations or you can call in the life you want to live with ease, but you can't do both. Think about it this way, if you were already the six figure CEO, or already living in your dream home with your dream partner with your dream 10 dogs, or living whatever life you want, do you think that you would still be holding onto the idea that it's not possible for you? That you're not good enough, worthy enough, it's too hard, or any other excuse your ego throws at you. Of course not. Because you're already living it. Will there be other thoughts at that new level that your ego tries to throw at you? Yes. Of course. That comes with the territory of being a human being.

You already know that what you focus on expands and what you're focusing on and thinking on a daily basis is being created in your physical reality. Simply put, those old thoughts will not create the life you want, they will only recreate the life you already have.

This means if you want to overcome self-sabotage, you put the self-sabotaging behaviors and thoughts through a filter. And the filter is that life you want to be living and choosing to see yourself through that filter as if you are already living it. As soon as a self-sabotaging behavior comes up, ask yourself, is this something that the best version of me is doing? If the answer is no, ask yourself what they would be doing instead.

Another way to look at this is through your values. What does the best possible version of yourself value? If a behavior or thought doesn't line up with those values, find ones that do. And continue to do this. Disrupt your thoughts and patterns consistently and you will begin to notice the self-sabotage less and less. Self-sabotage will push you down the chute if you let it but you have the power every single day to recognize when it's happening and choose the thoughts, beliefs, and behaviors that will get you to where you want to go.

When You Notice Self-Sabotage Come Up (or even when you don't but you're not getting what you want) Ask Yourself these Questions:

- Is what I'm doing/who I am being/what I am thinking right now getting me closer to where I want to be or pushing me further away?
- What could I do differently/what characteristics could I embody to help me overcome these behaviors and make better choices? (committed, disciplined, focused, etc.)
- What am I valuing right now that isn't in alignment with my goals?
- How is this behavior serving me? (You wouldn't be doing it if it wasn't serving you in some way even if that is just that it's distracting you)
- How can I make this task/project more fun and enjoyable?
- Is this the best place for my limited time and focus to be spent?
- Who can I forgive today and release myself of past pain and hurt?
- If you're noticing resistance around forgiveness, ask yourself this; what do I believe it would mean if I let go and forgive this person or situation? Can I change the meaning of it?

"You can play the "what if" game if you want, but at least rig it in your favor."

CHAPTER 19

FEEL THE FEAR AND DO IT ANYWAY

In the summer of 2003, I walked into a small downtown shop with my mom and as I strolled the aisles, not so patiently hanging on her arm while pleading with her to please hurry up I'm bored, when there, on a shelf, I saw it. A beautiful purple journal with a black spine and a white cut out on the front with two dragonflies perched perfectly in mid-air. She was beautiful. I was drawn to her like a fly to a light on a porch. I picked her up and felt the soft purple fabric on the palms of my hands. I ran my fingers through the pages and thought about all the words that would one day fill it. I had no idea that this journal would set the stage for my life in a way that I could never have imagined.

That very night, I crawled up the stairs of my wooden bunk bed with my new journal under my arm. I could feel the excitement bubbling in my chest as I sat under the covers with my flashlight and cracked open the journal. I grabbed my favorite blue gel pen and began to write my very first journal entry. I'd like to say it was something so profound you'd find it as an inspirational quote in a prestigious library somewhere in the world, but it wasn't. To be honest it was about how I thought going to the bathroom was a waste of time and energy and I didn't want to do it anymore. I was only 11 at the time and bathroom stories were apparently profound to me at that age. Later I adorned the once pristine cover with "inspirational quotes" and sayings such as, "It's a chick's world…but it's just better with dudes." and, "ROCK ON!" and, "Shit happens, we all gotta deal". "Hope, love and happiness". Along with all the boys' names I thought I was in love with.

As I hold the journal in my hands now, it's like opening a time capsule to how my life was all those years ago. The journal is littered with stories, tear stains, pictures of the Backstreet boys, my hopes, my dreams, fears of my impending surgeries and the less profound, "homework sux" tribute. Some of the pages are taped together, others are filled with sloppy handwriting and a whole bunch of scribbled out words. Some of the stories make me cry and shake my head wishing I could wrap my 11-year-old self up in a bear hug and tell her everything will be okay. Other stories make my whole-body cringe with intense feeling. And then there are the stories that make me laugh out loud. One of those big belly laughs, like, what was I thinking?!

No matter what I was going through, that journal was there for me, and for two whole years I wrote it all down. Oftentimes in bed long after I was supposed to be sawing logs. Other times I sat on my window sill looking out at the neighborhood before me, using my giant teddy bear as a back rest while I furiously scribbled in my new journal. She was a friend to me. A solace from the world. There was nothing like that first taste of writing for me. Once I started, I was hooked. Writing gave me the freedom I needed from the thoughts that were constantly building a nest inside my head. Writing allowed me to put those thoughts onto paper and begin the process of untangling them like a ball of yarn in a bowl.

I had no idea that that first journal would light a fire inside me so bright, it has yet to be burned out. Though it's been dimmed many times. I can still remember the first time I ever thought about writing a book. It wasn't even a thought really, it was more of a voice declaring what was to come. "I am an author and my book will be in bookstores across the world." Back then it was a dream. Just something a little girl said alone to herself in her room, perched on her window seat, scribbling in her purple journal. Even though the dream itself never went away as the years went on, my dreams of one day becoming a published author began to fade. The encouraging words I once heard were drowned out by, "Who do you think you are?", "Why would anyone read your book?" "You'll never even get the opportunity." Among other things.

I understand now something I didn't know back then; those words and thoughts rolling around inside my head were voices of my insecurities, my worries, my fears. They were all bundled up, intertwining together to create something bigger than they were alone. They grew larger and louder the more attention I gave them. And they worked to keep me stuck, stagnant, frustrated, and longing for more. For years.

It's so easy to get frustrated at your ego. Wishing it away. Wishing life would just be easier. Even turning your ego into a villain. Which it isn't. It's harder to lean in and listen to what's being said. To take the words no matter how harsh, and chew on them like a dog with a bone, whittling them away, understanding them, and then releasing them. That's the scariest thing in the world to do - go up against your own mind. Because you're going against it without any armor or weapons or even a helmet. Tackling your ego isn't about putting on layers of protection, it's about taking off the years of "truths" and stories that aren't even your own. Taking off the people who hurt you, the guilt you feel, the pain of the past and most of all, the fear that's held you back for so many years. It's about doing it scared because the whole point is to do it anyway.

We so deeply fear the unknown because we truly believe there are only two options in life - success or failure. We forget that they are two paths that lead to the same road. You cannot have one without the other because you can only know success once you've experienced failure and you can only know failure once you've experienced success. No matter what path you decide to take, you will be given a result. Whether this result is what you want or not is up to you. You have two choices: allow your ego-based fear to control your life or look the fear in the eye and charge forward with the trust that you're going to make it out better than when you went in.

Looking back, I also recognize something else; none of it matters now. All those fears I once had about the boys that didn't like me back, the petty arguments with my brother, the fear of not being enough or being too much, the fear of chasing a dream that would never be realized, or anything in between doesn't even matter anymore because everything worked out in the long run. So often we are looking at our fears from the perspective of the bottom of the mountain. We run around looking for all these things we think we need before we can get to the top. We focus on how long the journey is. If we'll ever even get there. We focus on the lack of external resources and believe we need to do something more to have what we want. This is ego-based thinking. The fear of not knowing how to get there, the fear of failing and not making it to the top, the fear of not having the right "equipment", the fear of what it means about who we are. This book is about helping you switch your focus and change your perspective about what you see in your life around you. Whether that means climbing a real-life mountain, leaving your job to pursue the business of your dreams, asking out your cute neighbor for dinner, or saying yes to a life changing opportunity that you've always wanted. The only thing holding you back from getting what you want out of life is the belief that something is holding you back. And that my friend is your ego talking.

It's time to stop fighting for your limitations, stop fighting for your ego's stories, stop fighting for the people, thoughts, feelings, and actions that are holding you back from living as your biggest, brightest and most authentic self. The thing is, your ego will always pop up. And that's okay because there are lessons to be found within the stories your ego plasters in your head and when you learn the lesson, you do something different. You show up different. You are different. And because of that, you get different results in your life.

Overcoming your ego is going to require you to throw more love at yourself than you ever have before. Look at your fears for what they truly are and choose something else. Find the comfort in the discomfort and even enjoy the feeling of being uncomfortable because that means you're growing. It's going to require you to rewrite the stories you've been holding onto so tightly that your hands are sore. It's going to require you to suspend your disbelief in what is possible for you and to trust that everything is rigged in your favor because it's not just you working on your life. But most importantly, it's going to require you to decide the life you want and who you want to be, and step into that version of you on a mental, physical, and spiritual level trusting that you'll either get a lesson that helps you get to the next level, or you'll get exactly what you asked for and even more than you could ever imagine.

The ending of this book marks the beginning of a beautiful, crazy, stupid scary, joyful and lesson filled journey for you. I don't have all the answers for you. I can't tell you what to do in every scenario possible. It'd be boring if I could and you'd be here for a really long time. I can only shed some light on the path. It's up to you to pick up your walking stick and move forward into the unknown knowing full well your ego is going to speak up - she will fight and claw her way through this but you're so much stronger than the mean girl in your head.

It would have been so easy for me to allow my big dreams to be swallowed whole by my ego like a monster underneath my bed. It would have been easier to ignore that soft nudge pushing me towards something else. Something greater. It would have been easier for me to make excuses, blame my circumstances, and pretend my dreams didn't matter because I never won anyway. That's what your ego will do to your dreams if you let her. She will distort them in such a way to make you believe it's not possible for you. It's been done too many times before. And if you allow her to speak up, she will. If you use the techniques you learned in this book, you will be able to face her head on and tell her, I believe I am capable of so much more.

Your story might not start with a dusty old journal or a profound experience that led you to choose a life bigger than the one you're living. And while I don't know your story yet, I do know this. Today you are going to do something you've never done before. You're going to listen to your heart over your head. Maybe it'll only be for a few seconds but that's okay because you are choosing to do something scary. You are choosing to look your ego in the face and ask yourself, "what are you trying to teach me?" instead of, "why are you doing this to me?". You are choosing to rewrite your own story right here and right now because you have all the tools you need to do so.

Whether you're feeling like your own biggest cheerleader or not, I want to leave you with this. I want you to get that promotion. I want you to make more money today than you ever have before. I want you to get that person that you've been crushing on. I want life to show you a miracle bigger than anything you could ever imagine. And if all you can do today is get out of bed and put on some pants, I want you to know that you are beautiful, you are loved, and I am rooting for you. Now it's time to root for yourself. And when you notice your ego popping up, you have the choice to look her in the face and say, not today. I choose to see it differently.

Guiding Questions to Live Your Best Life

Use these questions to help yourself understand and uncover where you're going and what you want out of life without your ego playing a role in your decisions. Remember the answer to these questions when your ego does pop up and try to crash your party. Doing so will help you stand your ground because the life you're looking to live is so much juicier than anything your ego can cook up because yes, you can have everything you want and so much more.

What do I want?

Don't shy away from this and really dig deep into what you want out of life. Not what your family wants, not what your friends want, not what the media wants or what's expected of you, and especially not what's "realistic". If you could be, do, have anything, what is your answer? What does your life look like?

Who do I Need to Be to Have What I Want?

This is the key. Who are you "being" will get you a lot further than what you are doing. This means, do you need to be someone who is committed? Someone who values self-integrity? Someone who is resourceful? When you embody the characteristic of the version of yourself who has what you want, you automatically value what they value and create the habits that will help you get there.

What Stories Can I Rewrite?

Everything is a story and it's either keeping you exactly where you are or moving you forward. These stories often come to you when you're not looking. They're the words that just pop out when you're not thinking. They're the first thoughts that pop into your head, the beliefs that don't align with what you want. Get clear on the stories that are not serving you and begin to rewrite them with stories that do serve you.

What/Who Can I Let Go Of?

While most of this work is done on the mental and spiritual level, some of it also needs to be done on a physical level as well. This comes down to certain habits and even people that are simply holding you back. If you want to be rich, but you spend most of your time with people who talk about how broke they are, it's going to be a lot harder for you to get what you want. Same with habits that keep you playing small. Take note of the physical things in your life that it's time to let go of as well as the past hurts that are holding you back.

How Will I Know When I Get There & What Will I Do to Celebrate?

If you can live your best life in your head first, it will be that much easier to have it come into your physical reality. Remember, everything starts as a picture in your head. This is how your subconscious knows where to take you. Having a clear picture of when you will know when you've reached wherever it is you want to go can help you create an even more vivid picture in your mind. Think about it like this; you're planning a trip to Australia. When does it feel real to you? When you've booked the tickets? When you're on the plane? When you're being greeted at your hotel? When you're snorkeling in the Great Barrier Reef? There are no right or wrong answers here but it's important for you to know.

Not only that but how will you celebrate? So often we're so focused on where we're going, we forget to take a minute and celebrate how far we've come. Close the circle. Celebrate yourself even if it's just for a few minutes. Just make sure to do it!

How do I want to Feel?

Most of the time, you want something because you believe it will make you feel a certain way. The money which will make you happy. The car which will make you feel rich. The significant other which will make you feel loved. Or so you're taught to believe. But as you know, you can choose to feel all of those feelings now and when you create the feelings for yourself instead of waiting for something outside of yourself to give them to you - they're going to last and it's going to mean more. So, how do you want whatever it is you want to make you feel? Happy? Abundant? Rich? Loved? Get very clear on this and then think about what you can do right now to get into those feelings. What can you do right now that will make you feel loved? Maybe that's taking yourself out on a date. Taking a bath with some candles (keeping it PG13 here). Figure out what you can do to feel those feelings now and feel them on a daily and consistent basis. This is another trick to help the Law of Attraction to work as well.

How can I get into Alignment with my Best Life?

Alignment - another buzz word. It really means aligning your thoughts, beliefs, and actions with what you desire to have in your life and making it really fun and easy. There are many ways to do this but the easiest is to simply address the thoughts you have coming up, ask yourself if they are hurting you or helping you, change them to thoughts that do help you, create values that align with the goals you want, and show up with the thoughts, beliefs, habits, and actions of someone who has what you want.

Also take note of your feelings and feel what you want to feel from the outcome. Abundant, safe, secure, happy, etc. The point isn't to be perfect at this but to have fun with it and make it a game. Do the best you can each and every day and you will watch as your life changes before your eyes.

Am I Open to Receiving?

It's so easy to forget that there is one final step to living the life you want and that is being open to receiving it. I mean duh, why wouldn't you be open to it right? But think about it. If you needed $1,000 dollars to pay rent this month and a family member gave you the money, how open would you be to taking it? Would you feel weird? Uncomfortable? Like there's a catch? It's the same when the pieces of your dream life begin to fall into place. Trust that you are 100% deserving of all the good that's coming to you, trust that it's meant for you, and be open to everything falling into place in a different way than you had it planned out in your head. If you ever feel like you're not receiving what you want, ask yourself, "What can I do right now to get into alignment with receiving?" Listen to what comes up.

"What's scarier; doing that thing that you've been putting off and stepping into the person you want to be or the story you've created about how you think it's supposed to go or what it means about who you are?"

ABOUT EMILY SYRING

Emily is an American author living in the Midwest. She is an NLP Practitioner, an EFT Practitioner, a clinical hypnotherapist, and a life and success coach specializing in mindset and manifestation. You can learn more about Emily online via her personal development blog, She's Living Her Best Life at sheslivingherbestlife.com.